1862

A SHORT HISTORY
OF THE LABOUR PARTY

By the same author

THE ORIGINS OF THE LABOUR PARTY

THE CHALLENGE OF SOCIALISM

AMERICA AND THE BRITISH LEFT

LABOUR AND POLITICS, 1900–1906
(with Frank Bealey)

THE BRITISH COMMUNIST PARTY

MODERN BRITAIN, 1885–1955

AMERICAN LABOR

A HISTORY OF BRITISH TRADE UNIONISM

SOCIAL GEOGRAPHY OF BRITISH ELECTIONS,
1895–1910

POPULAR POLITICS AND SOCIETY
IN LATE VICTORIAN BRITAIN

BRITAIN AND THE SECOND WORLD WAR

WINSTON CHURCHILL

THE LABOUR GOVERNMENTS, 1945–1951

BRITAIN AND THE MARSHALL PLAN

A SHORT HISTORY
OF THE
LABOUR PARTY

HENRY PELLING

Fellow of St John's College, Cambridge

TENTH EDITION

St. Martin's Press

© Henry Pelling 1961, 1965, 1968, 1972, 1976, 1978, 1982, 1985, 1991, 1993

First published in Great Britain 1961 by
THE MACMILLAN PRESS LTD
Houndmills, Basingstoke, Hampshire RG21 2XS
and London
Companies and representatives
throughout the world

A catalogue record for this book is available
from the British Library.

ISBN 0–333–59475–4 hardcover
ISBN 0–333–59476–2 paperback

Printed in Hong Kong

Reprinted 1961 (twice), 1962; Second Edition 1965; Third Edition 1968;
Fourth Edition 1972, Reprinted 1974; Fifth Edition 1976; Sixth Edition 1978;
Seventh Edition 1982, Reprinted 1983; Eighth Edition 1985, Reprinted 1986,
1989; Ninth Edition 1991, Reprinted 1992; Tenth Edition 1993, Reprinted 1994

First published in the United States of America 1972 by
Scholarly and Reference Division,
ST. MARTIN'S PRESS, INC.,
175 Fifth Avenue,
New York, N.Y. 10010

ISBN 0–312–09676–3

Library of Congress Cataloging-in-Publication Data
Pelling, Henry.
A short history of the labour party / Henry Pelling — 10th ed.
p.   cm.
Includes index.
ISBN 0–312–09676–3
1. Labour Party (Great Britain)—History.   I. Title.
JN1129.L32P42   1993
324.24107—dc20   93–16705
                                            CIP

CONTENTS

LIST OF ILLUSTRATIONS

The photographs of Arthur Henderson and Aneurin Bevan and
Hugh Gaitskell are by the *Daily Herald*. That of James Callaghan and
Harold Wilson is Crown Copyright. That of Michael Foot and Neil
Kinnock is reproduced by permission of the *The Times*. That of John
Smith is reproduced by permission of the *Independent*. The others are
from the B.B.C. Hulton Picture Library.

CHAPTER I

The New Party: Ideal and Reality
(to 1906)

(1)

THE Labour Party is as old as the twentieth century, in fact if not in name. Its foundation took place at a conference in London in February 1900, and its later annual conferences are numbered from this date forward. But until just after the general election of January 1906, the party's activities were conducted under the more modest title of the 'Labour Representation Committee'.

How did the Labour Representation Committee (or L.R.C. as we must call it) come into existence, and how did it succeed in transforming itself into a Labour Party? The long-term reasons were complex. It was partly because the enfranchisement of the manual workers in 1867 and in 1884 tended to increase the electoral importance of 'labour' and its leaders. But this factor by itself would not have been enough, as we know from our observation of American politics. Why was 'labour' a more or less homogeneous force in British politics, at least at the turn of the century? And why could it not adapt one or other of the existing parties to its purposes? The answer to the first of these additional questions takes us into the realm of the sociologist and economic historian; but it may be tentatively suggested that various social and economic changes were in the later nineteenth century leading in the direction of a greater solidarity of manual workers, partly by raising the standards of the unskilled workers to a level somewhat closer to that of the artisans, and partly by depressing, or at least threatening, the relative position of the artisans; and also by the gradual weakening of the local, regional and religious characteristics of the country which had contributed so much to the differentiation between the existing political parties. As for the failure to adopt one or other of these parties to the purposes of 'labour', the explanation must be found in the peculiarities of their organisation, and particularly that of the Liberal Party, to which the larger proportion of labour leaders belonged: it seems that the Liberal associations in the constituencies were too inflexible to adapt themselves to the rise of a new social class.

Early in the nineteenth century, there had been little concept of 'labour' as a single distinct class in the community. As Professor Asa Briggs has shown, it was more usual to speak of 'the labouring classes' or 'the middle classes' in the plural, thus recognising the variety to be found under both descriptions. During the 1870's and 1880's, however, the concept of a single 'working class', as also of a single 'middle class', began to develop. The Education Act of 1870 tended to separate the population more clearly into those who were educated at their parents' expense and those who went to the 'Board' schools or the church schools; nearly all the manual workers fell into the latter category. Furthermore, from the 1880's the unskilled workers were able to imitate the artisans in forming unions of their own, which were accepted into the company of the societies of the skilled men by being admitted to the Trades Union Congress. At the same time, the 'trades' themselves were being transformed by the mechanisation of industry and the growth of the scale of production: factory work replaced the work of the individual craftsman in more and more occupations as the 'industrial revolution' slowly spread through industries which had remained almost unchanged in their basic processes for centuries — shoemaking, for instance, or printing, which were both much affected in this period; and the close personal contact and collaboration between master and workman became a thing of the past. Thus it was that the unskilled

2

labourer, concerned to achieve some minimum standards for himself and his family and to safeguard himself against unemployment, found allies in the ranks of the disgruntled artisans. Some of both groups took up with Socialism — a creed advocating a complete transformation of capitalist society, and often as in William Morris's writings hinting at a return to the age of the independent craftsman — but in the 1880's and 1890's it was in fact only a tiny minority of the so-called 'working class' which had as yet responded to 'the cause'. Like most new political faiths, Socialism started out as the enthusiasm of a few middle-class leaders; and the comparative prosperity of the employed workers in the late nineteenth century limited the success of the Socialists' appeal.

If its Socialist enthusiasm was not strong, why did the newly enfranchised 'working class', with its growing homogeneity, fail to infiltrate and capture the bastions of an existing political party, and in particular, the Liberal Party? Certainly the Liberal Party seemed likely to be open to some such infiltration, for it was already a coalition of political forces whose relative strength varied from time to time, and it contained a radical wing which had made a strong appeal for working-class support. Unfortunately, however, in the 1870's and 1880's its structure had become rather rigid, and its leadership lacked both the power and the will to alter the situation. The local Liberal associations, largely in the hands of business and professional men and Nonconformist ministers, would rarely adopt working men as candidates, partly because they would have to take on the burden of paying the election expenses and upkeep of a poor man, and partly because their own special interests would suffer if the 'labour question' were thrust to the fore. The ageing Gladstone, obsessed with his 'mission' to 'pacify Ireland', would not take up the questions which seemed vital to young labour leaders, such as the state payment of M.P.s; and it was against his principles to venture into the vast field of social legislation if he could possibly avoid it.

As a result of all this, in 1893 an Independent Labour Party was formed at Bradford with the object of sending working men to Parliament, independent of both the Liberal and Conservative Parties. Its leaders admitted that they had been impressed by the success of the Irish Nationalists under Parnell in concentrating the attention of the major parties on the Irish question; they hoped to do the same thing for questions of social reform. The new body adopted a Socialist constitution, but, as can be seen from its name, it expected to win support from the workers whether they were Socialists or not. Several of its early leaders were men whose main objection to the Liberal Party was that it had failed to adopt them as Liberal candidates. This was the case with Keir Hardie, the Scottish miner who sat as an Independent Labour M.P. in the 1892 Parliament and who came to be regarded as the embodiment of the I.L.P. idea. The organisation also drew strength from the members of the new unions of the unskilled, who feared that without some sort of legislative assistance their industrial gains would be swept away in the next trade depression. After its foundation, the party also drew support from those who were disappointed with the Liberal Party after Gladstone's retirement. For when the 'Grand Old Man' at last retired in 1894, his successor, chosen by Queen Victoria, was Lord Rosebery, a young aristocrat with little popular appeal, whose most remarkable success was to win the Derby twice during his premiership (a remarkable feat, as his government lasted for only fifteen months), and who later emerged as a strong supporter of British imperial expansion in Africa and elsewhere.

Yet in 1899–1900, when the inauguration of the Labour Representation Committee was actually being undertaken, the I.L.P. and the other Socialist organisations (the Social-Democratic Federation and the Fabian Society) were pitiably weak, and as imperialism became the major issue of British politics they had been rapidly losing members. The country was in the grip of a jingoistic fervour which rose to a climax in the South African War; and the Socialists suffered, not only because their primary concern was with domestic politics, but also because in most cases they actively opposed the war. To understand why it was that the Trade Union Congress agreed in the summer of 1899 to sponsor a meeting on labour representation, and also why the delegates who attended the resulting conference in February 1900 did manage to agree on the establishment of permanent machinery, we must turn to an examination of trade-union vicissitudes in the course of the 1890's.

(2)

In the last decade of the nineteenth century there were many reasons to make trade unionists and especially their officials feel insecure and anxious to obtain direct parliamentary representation. There had been a strong employers' reaction against the sudden expansion of unionism at the end of the 1880's, and this led them to search for every possible method of turning the tide. At the same time, the growth of industry, its national consolidation, and its new forms of organisation were all factors making for uncertainty in industrial relations. It was easy to believe, however, that the undermining of the legal position of the unionism as understood since the acts of the 1870's was due to a deliberate attempt to crush trade unionism.

Certainly the foundation in 1893 of a National Free Labour Association, to supply 'blacklegs' to take the place of workmen on strike, was a direct attack on unionism. But this body was not in fact very successful and its main influence was often to strengthen the resolve of strikers rather than to beat down their resistance. More important as a permanent threat was the growth of national federations of employers: the best example was the Federation of Engineering Employers, which in 1897–8 conducted the first national strike or lock-out, that of the engineering firms against the Amalgamated Society of Engineers. Worried by the success of German and American competition, the employers were inclined to think that the best way to improve their competitive position was to reduce costs by reducing wages, and they observed with envy the comparative weakness of unionism in other countries, particularly in the United States. In 1898 the further important step was taken of forming an Employers' Parliamentary Council, which was designed to promote the interests of employers generally at Westminster.

The legal rights of trade unions, up to the 1890's, had apparently been defined by the Trade Union Acts of 1871 and 1876 and the Conspiracy and Protection of Property Act, 1875. But a series of lawsuits in the 1890's changed the situation, and because these cases were sometimes finally decided by the House of Lords as the final arbiter, labour leaders often jumped to the conclusion that these decisions were political in character. It is certainly possible that political considerations influenced the judges, just as in America the Supreme Court is said to 'follow the election returns'. But the willingness of the Lords in their judicial capacity to allow trade unions to be sued for the tortious acts of their officials — something which the union officials had thought to be impossible under earlier legislation — unquestionably owed a good deal to the general development of company law, and particularly to the appearance of the device known as the 'representative action'. The law about union liability was not, however, finally decided in the 1890's; and at the turn of the century union officials were primarily concerned about their rights of picketing, now seriously restricted by a case known as *Lyons* v. *Wilkins*, which had gone no further than the Court of Appeal. If unionists could not picket, they were virtually powerless to carry on a strike effectively. The Employers' Parliamentary Council interested itself in this decision, and issued a statement to its members pointing out that picketing had now become 'almost harmless'.

It was in this situation that the 1899 Trade Union Congress, meeting as usual in September, had to consider a resolution from the Amalgamated Society of Railway Servants to summon a special conference of trade unions,

co-operative societies, and Socialist bodies in order to make
plans for labour representation in Parliament. The proposal had come originally from the Doncaster branch of
the Railway Servants, where it had been put forward by
an I.L.P. member, Thomas R. Steels, who had served a
term on the union's national executive. As a Socialist, he
wanted to see the new organisation keep clear of the existing political parties, and his resolution was completely in
line with the policy of Keir Hardie and the other leaders of
the I.L.P. The support of the T.U.C. might not have been
forthcoming, however, if the resolution had been too out-
spoken on the question of political independence. As it
was, it was hotly debated, and opposed by the miners, who
could already by virtue of the concentration of membership
in particular areas elect M.P.s without help from other
unions, forcing the Liberal Party to accept their candidates.
(These were the so-called 'Lib-Labs'.) Nevertheless, the
resolution was carried, by 546,000 votes against 434,000.
About a third of the delegates must have abstained from
voting, and to judge by those who spoke in the debate, the
main supporters were the leaders of the new unskilled
unions, who evidently hoped that parliamentary representation would be a valuable safeguard of the future existence of their organisations.

After the Congress was over, there was some conflict
between the conservative T.U.C. Parliamentary Committee
— which represented the T.U.C. in between meetings of
Congress — and the Socialist leaders as to who should make
the arrangements for the conference on labour representation, and how the agenda should be drawn up. But the
conference finally met on 27th and 28th February 1900,
in the Memorial Hall, near Ludgate Circus, and this
meeting has always been looked upon as 'the foundation
of the Labour Party'. Yet at the time it was not looked
upon as having accomplished this. All that the delegates
did was to establish a committee to promote and co-ordinate
plans for labour representation: something comparable
with the Labour Representation League of 1869, or the

Labour Electoral Committee of 1886. The financial arrangements made to support the committee were very limited and simple : organisations affiliated to it were to pay no more than 10s. per thousand members, and on such a basis the committee could neither appoint any paid official nor finance any candidatures of its own. No political programme was agreed upon and it was not even decided whether the new body was to work in collaboration with one or other of the existing political parties, as its predecessors had done, or to establish an independent party of its own.

As nobody seemed to want the job, the I.L.P. had no difficulty in securing the secretaryship for their nominee, Ramsay MacDonald, then a young journalist. It was also fortunate that Frederick Rogers, the first chairman of the executive, though not a Socialist, was at least keen to see the new body established on a firm footing. Rogers drastically altered Keir Hardie's draft for the organisation's first circular, as he put it, 'with an eye to the oldfashioned trade unionist, who if he cannot push us forward may be a very dead weight indeed to hold us back'.[1] Even the moderation of Rogers, however, could make no impact on the co-operative leaders, and after attending the national co-operative conference in 1900 he declared that he was 'hardly prepared for the solid unbending Toryism of the older men, and the meek acquiescence or flippant contempt of the younger ones, in relation to social affairs'.[2] Under these circumstances, the committee had to abandon hope of winning the support of the co-operative societies.

There were, of course, obvious technical reasons why even the most 'advanced' unions might be slow to join. Their constitutions imposed cumbersome delays in making decisions, and although some secretaries or executive councils were empowered to take action of this character, it was more commonly thought necessary or desirable to consult the membership by referendum or to leave the matter to an annual or biennial conference. Where a referendum was undertaken, the apathy of the membership militated against a clear-cut decision, for a majority in a very small poll was not always regarded as binding. George Barnes, the secretary of the Amalgamated Society of Engineers, and himself a member of the I.L.P., was forced to write to the L.R.C. to say that 'the members of the Society have evinced so little interest in the question of Parliamentary representation that we cannot see how we can take part'.[3]

Generally speaking, the unions which joined in the first year were the new unions of the unskilled, partly because their constitutions tended to be more centralised, and partly because their officers were more inclined to believe in political action — several of them in fact being Socialists. In addition, however, there was the Amalgamated Society of Railway Servants, which had initiated the conference by its T.U.C. resolution and which stood to gain very much by representation in Parliament, where so much railway legislation was discussed and enacted. If we add the two main printers' unions and the Boot and Shoe Workers — all of whom were suffering from rapid technological change and who seem to have been in a particularly radical mood — we have accounted for about two-thirds of the union membership of the Labour Representation Committee at the end of its first year.

In addition, of course, there were the Socialist societies : the I.L.P., the Social-Democratic Federation or S.D.F. (a Marxist group), and the Fabians. These bodies had by decision of the inaugural conference secured representation on the committee out of all proportion to their membership and financial contribution. The Fabians had one seat and the other bodies two seats each : thus they had five seats out of a total of twelve on the committee, and in addition the secretary of the committee, the only full-time (albeit unpaid) officer of the organisation, was a nominee of the I.L.P. Yet the Socialist societies in the first year provided only about 6 per cent of the funds. The charges of Socialist dictation and control of the new organisation would certainly have had a great deal of substance, if it had not been that the three societies were at odds with one another. The

S.D.F., dissatisfied at the refusal of the inaugural conference and of the conference a year later to accept the 'class war' concept, retired from membership and their two seats on the committee disappeared; and Edward Pease, the Fabian representative, opposed the I.L.P. attempt to make the L.R.C. into a new political party and found himself on the 'unionist' as against the 'Socialist' side on nearly all issues of disagreement. Much continued to depend, therefore, upon the enthusiasm of the non-Socialist union leaders for this new form of political action.

(3)

The first general election fought by the L.R.C. took place only six months after its inauguration. When the Unionist government dissolved in the summer, the crisis of the South African War had just been surmounted, and it could expect to benefit from the wave of patriotic enthusiasm then affecting all classes — and not least the working class. Fifteen candidates sponsored by individual unions or by Socialist societies were endorsed by the L.R.C., although the L.R.C. could not do more for them than provide a small supply of leaflets and its best wishes. The total L.R.C. expenditure on the general election amounted to only £33. Under these circumstances, it was more the result of its good fortune than of its efforts that two of its candidates were returned to Parliament. At Derby, Richard Bell, the secretary of the Railway Servants, was elected in the company of a Liberal for a two-member seat; and at Merthyr, Keir Hardie had the same experience. Hardie, it may be said, owed his success entirely to the fortunate coincidence that the Welsh miners opposed the South African War, while one of the two Liberals seeking re-election at Merthyr did not.

With only two M.P.s, however, the L.R.C. could not make much impression in Parliament, especially as Bell and Hardie were not very compatible. Hardie was a Socialist who favoured an independent stand on many questions;

Bell was virtually nothing but a Liberal except on questions of direct importance to his union, the Railway Servants. The general election also returned several 'Lib-Labs' — only eight, as against twelve at the dissolution, but enough to prevent the two L.R.C. men from being regarded as representative of Labour in general. Consequently, although the L.R.C. could claim the election results as creditable, it could not hope that they would do much to convince unaffiliated unions of the importance of joining their ranks.

What really strengthened the willingness of trade-union officers to recommend affiliation to the L.R.C. was the Taff Vale judgment by the House of Lords in July 1901. This decision emerged from a strike on the Taff Vale railway in 1900, during which the general manager of the railway company, following the advice of the Employers' Parliamentary Council, brought actions for damages against the Secretary of the Railway Servants for picketing the Cardiff stations. The judgment reaffirmed *Lyons* v. *Wilkins* on picketing and also declared that the union's funds were liable for the tortious acts of its officials. The Taff Vale Railway Company could go ahead and secure damages from the Railway Servants, and in fact a total of £23,000 had to be paid — a figure which included the company's costs, but not the union's.

As was to be expected, the impact of such a complicated legal decision caused much confusion, but most union leaders soon began to realise that they had suffered a serious setback in their ceaseless struggle against the employers. Although they continued to press the existing parties in the House of Commons to pass legislation restoring the *status quo ante* Taff Vale, and although they found the Liberal Party (which was of course in opposition) to be generally favourable, they also moved in increasing numbers to the support of the Labour Representation Committee, which promised to help them to elect their own members as M.P.s. Consequently the L.R.C. membership rose from 376,000 early in 1901 to 469,000 a year later and 861,000 in 1903.

11

The largest reinforcements came from the adhesion of the Textile Workers — a group of unions with altogether more than a hundred thousand members. This occurred largely as the result of a by-election in the weaving constituency of Clitheroe, where the secretary of the Cotton Weavers, David Shackleton, was adopted by the L.R.C. Philip Snowden, who was being considered as an I.L.P. candidate, won much credit by withdrawing in Shackleton's favour. The union's strength in the constituency was so great that although it had previously been a Liberal seat, neither the Liberals nor the Conservatives felt able to challenge Shackleton's return, albeit he described himself simply as a Labour candidate. Shackleton's unopposed success was followed by a ballot of the Textile Workers to decide whether they favoured parliamentary representation, and on the affirmative result of the ballot the Textile Workers early in 1903 joined the L.R.C. in a body. The Engineers had also joined in the course of 1902, after the prolonged constitutional wrestling that always seemed to be necessary for major decisions in this union. As a result, the only large unions not yet in the L.R.C. were those of the miners, whose success in electing their own members as 'Lib-Labs' continued to inhibit their enthusiasm for joining in with the other unions or abandoning the Liberal Party.

With all this additional support, the L.R.C. at its third conference at Newcastle in February 1903 was able to consolidate itself and tighten its constitution. The subscription rate was increased and furthermore a compulsory parliamentary fund was established for the payment of M.P.s. The result was that the payment made by the affiliated unions and Socialist societies went up from 10s. per thousand members to almost £5. The payment of M.P.s obviously provided an effective way of asserting discipline over Members of Parliament and candidates; and the conference could expect to be obeyed when it also decided that henceforth its candidates must 'strictly abstain from identifying themselves with or promoting the interests of any section of the Liberal or Conservative parties'.

These changes added a great deal both to the strength and to the independence of the L.R.C., making it more of a new 'party' than ever before. Yet at the same time they increased the eagerness of the Liberal Chief Whip, Herbert Gladstone, to come to some terms with the L.R.C. The expectation of an early general election, owing to disagreements in the Unionist Cabinet about Tariff Reform, increased the urgency of the matter. Accordingly, Gladstone and Ramsay MacDonald secretly negotiated an agreement to enable the L.R.C. to put up most of its candidates without the need to face Liberal opposition.

The Unionist Government did not fall in 1903, and so the danger of an immediate election was averted. Even so, the agreement between MacDonald and Gladstone was confirmed and, although secret, was remarkably effective in avoiding clashes between L.R.C. and Liberal candidates — at least in England, but not in Scotland where the writ of the National Liberal Federation did not run. This was in spite of the enthusiasm of local organisations on both sides — Liberal associations and local L.R.C.s — to put up candidates and make a fight against all comers. On the side of the L.R.C., probably only Keir Hardie was fully in the know about the agreement, and local branches of the I.L.P. were particularly embarrassing in their demands for contests. They could, however, largely be held in check by lack of financial backing from the centre and by the argument that the I.L.P. could not claim more than a proportion of the total L.R.C. candidatures.

It was fortunate, moreover, that the rapprochement of Liberal and Socialist opinion, which had begun when both the Radicals and the I.L.P. opposed the South African War, was confirmed by the new issues raised by the Unionists during their remaining term of office. Both Liberals and L.R.C. supporters (the Fabians alone excepted) could unite in opposition to the 1902 Education Act, which seemed to damage the interests of the Nonconformists; both too could denounce the Chamberlain plan for Tariff Reform, which from 1903 onwards rapidly became the leading political controversy of the time. Both also found an emotive if somewhat ephemeral slogan in 'Chinese labour', for the introduction of Chinese indentured labour in South Africa was alarming both on humanitarian grounds and on the grounds of the competition that it would afford with British emigrant labour.

Meanwhile the L.R.C. was able to establish a record of by-election successes, which more and more convinced the Liberals of the value of co-operation. Following the un-opposed success at Clitheroe, in March 1903 Will Crooks, a popular Cockney working man, with Liberal support won a straight fight against a Unionist candidate at Woolwich: this victory strengthened MacDonald's hand in his negotiations with Herbert Gladstone. In May of the same year, John Hodge, the secretary of the Steel Smelters, polled un-expectedly well, although unsuccessfully, in the Tory strong-hold of Preston; and in July Arthur Henderson of the Ironfounders won a seat from the Liberals in a three-cor-nered contest at Barnard Castle. The return of Crooks and Henderson as well as Shackleton brought the L.R.C. mem-bership of the Commons up to a theoretical total of five, but Bell was showing reluctance to abide by the require-ments of independence as stated at the L.R.C. conference of 1903, and in 1904 he was officially regarded as having lapsed from the group. As none of the recently elected trio was a Socialist or a keen independent, MacDonald and Hardie had a good deal of difficulty in keeping them on the narrow line of political separation from the Liberals: and indeed their task was all the harder in view of their own secret commitment to co-operation with the Liberals by the MacDonald-Gladstone electoral agreement.

(4)

When the election finally took place in January 1906, it was clear that MacDonald's plans for its conduct on the Labour side had worked out perfectly. The L.R.C. had in all fifty candidates, as it had intended; forty of them were sponsored by individual trade unions, by trades councils or

by local L.R.C.s, and a further ten were sponsored by the
I.L.P. Only eighteen of the fifty were opposed by Liberal
candidates, and of these eighteen, some faced only unofficial candidates on the Liberal side. In ten double-member
constituencies, one Liberal and one L.R.C. candidate fought
side by side against Conservative opposition. The co-operation between Liberals and the L.R.C. was most complete
in Lancashire, which had lately been a strong Conservative
area and which was not expected to show much change unless some such electoral alliance was effected. In Wales and
Yorkshire, on the other hand, where Liberalism remained
fairly strong, its leaders had felt less need for concessions to
Labour; in Scotland they made none at all.

If the main issue of the general election had been social
reform, it might have been possible to detect some conflict
between Liberal and L.R.C. candidates, and some difference between the electoral support that they obtained, in
spite of the electoral agreement. In fact, however, the
issues of the election were simply those which differentiated
most of the Liberals from the Conservatives: Tariff Reform,
'Chinese Labour', Education, and (a rather poor fourth)
Home Rule for Ireland. The tide ran strongly in the
direction of Liberalism, especially in Lancashire, where
Tariff Reform seemed to threaten the established foreign
markets of the cotton trade. The result was that the Liberals
secured 377 seats, giving them a majority of 84 over all
other parties combined. In the Liberal wake, the L.R.C.
secured 29 seats, no less than 12 of them being in Lancashire.

Of the twenty-nine L.R.C. men in the new Parliament,
seven, including Hardie, MacDonald, and Snowden, were
sponsored by the I.L.P. The remainder, although sponsored by trade unions or local labour bodies, also contained
a good many members of the I.L.P., and one (Will Thorne,
the secretary of the Gasworkers Union) was a member of
the S.D.F. It was equally significant, however, that of the
successful twenty-nine, only five were elected against Liberal
opposition, and at least two of these five had faced only
unofficial Liberal opposition. Two of the other three were

the L.R.C.'s sole representatives from Scotland. Altogether ten members — more than a third of the party — were elected in two-member constituencies, where the other member was a Liberal. All of the twenty-nine new M.P.s were of working-class origin, and this had in fact been true of all the fifty candidates, except for one, Stanton Coit, who was an American. Several of them were the secretaries of important unions — the Gasworkers, the Steel Smelters, the Shipwrights, and the Engineers — while others had had long careers as officials of unions; many of them were under a vague Socialist influence, but only one or two were Marxists. Most of them claimed to be devoutly religious — nearly all being some sort of Methodist, or Congregationalist.

The success of the L.R.C. created a sensation at the time, and Balfour, the defeated Unionist leader, went so far as to suggest that the new Liberal Prime Minister, Campbell-Bannerman, was a 'mere cork' on the Socialist tide. In reality, as even a few Socialists including Bernard Shaw pointed out at the time, it was largely the other way about: the L.R.C. was a cork on the Liberal tide, and if any 'ism' was triumphant in 1906 it was Gladstonianism.

NOTES

1. Rogers to MacDonald, 13 Mar. 1900, Labour Party Letter Files, Transport House.
2. Rogers to MacDonald, 30 May 1900, *ibid.*
3. Barnes to MacDonald, 7 Nov. 1900, *ibid.*

FURTHER READING

A fuller narrative and discussion of the issues raised in this chapter will be found in Henry Pelling, *Origins of the Labour Party, 1880–1900* (new ed., 1965), and in Frank Bealey and Henry Pelling, *Labour and Politics, 1900–6* (1958). A more succinct account, though weak on the industrial side, is Philip P. Poirier, *Advent of the Labour Party* (1958). There are important biographies of Keir Hardie by K. O. Morgan (1975) and of Ramsay MacDonald by David Marquand (1977).

The New Party: Ideal and Reality (to 1906)

G. D. H. Cole's *British Working Class Politics, 1832–1914* (1941) provides an outline of the electoral activity of labour. Some of the atmosphere of the period is effectively recreated in Joseph Clayton, *Rise and Decline of Socialism, 1884–1924* (1926), an undeservedly neglected book.

H. A. Clegg, A. Fox and A. F. Thompson, *History of British Trade Unionism since 1889*, i (Oxford, 1964), contains a full account of the unions' political activities, including the foundation and early history of the Labour Party.

CHAPTER II

A Pressure-group under Pressure
(1906–14)

(1)

As soon as the 1906 Parliament assembled, the L.R.C. assumed the name of 'Labour Party' and its twenty-nine M.P.s elected officers and whips. The life of the party in the following eight years, 1906–14, although undergoing many vicissitudes, yet has a certain unity for analytical purposes. The great tide of Liberal feeling, which had brought the Labour Party to Parliament, ebbed considerably, as was shown by the two elections in 1910; and the Labour Party, only too much like a cork, ebbed with it, and lost a few seats in the 1910 elections. The apparent increase in the number of Labour M.P.s — from twenty-nine in 1906 to forty after the first 1910 election and forty-two after the second 1910 election — is entirely accounted for by the accession of most of the miners' M.P.s, formerly 'Lib-Labs', after the Miners Federation decided to join the Labour Party in 1909. Furthermore, after the second 1910 election the Labour Party strength was reduced by the loss of by-elections, and at the outbreak of war numbered only thirty-seven, of whom twelve were miners' representatives. It will be seen, then, that the record of the parliamentary party in these eight years was not one of numerical advance in any real sense.

It would have been to the advantage of the Labour Party to dissociate itself from the Liberals, once it had a fairly strong representation in Parliament, and to devise its policies and propaganda on a basis of complete independence. The difficulties which prevented it from doing this, however, were numerous. First of all, there was the character of the parliamentary situation, which obliged the party to vote either for or against proposals of the Liberal government. After all, there are only two voting lobbies in the House, and abstention is not an impressive way of representing one's constituency. The fact that from 1908 onwards the Liberals, under pressure from Lloyd George, did take a strong initiative on social reform obliged the Labour Party either to support the Liberal policy or risk criticism as opponents of practicable reform. After the first 1910 election, moreover, the Labour Party lost what freedom of action it had retained in the preceding four years owing to the government's lack of a clear majority. The support of the Labour Party and the Irish was essential if the government was to stay in office; and owing to its special financial difficulties at the time, the Labour Party did not dare to risk a fresh dissolution — at least, not after the second 1910 election, which it survived only with considerable difficulty.

There was also the special problem created by the success of the MacDonald-Gladstone electoral pact. As we have seen, many of the Labour M.P.s owed their election to Liberal support, and this was particularly obvious in the two-member constituencies, where several of them had been returned in harness with a Liberal. When by-elections occurred, as they sometimes did, owing to the decease or promotion of the Liberal M.P. in one of these two-member constituencies, the parliamentary party and MacDonald himself (who represented the two-member constituency of Leicester) were extremely reluctant to contest the vacancy, much to the irritation of the local branches of the I.L.P.

At the same time, there was the fact that the Labour Party was largely deficient in parliamentary and administrative talent, and it was incapable of producing satisfactory alternative policies of reform. The Labour M.P.s, as has already been pointed out, were all of working-class origin, and though some of them were quite able men, they lacked professional training and administrative experience. They had as yet no middle-class Fabians in their ranks, and in any case they distrusted the Fabian leaders, especially the Webbs and Bernard Shaw, because of their readiness to 'permeate' the older political parties with their ideas. In particular, Sidney Webb had had a part in shaping the Education Act of 1902, of which most of the Labour Party disapproved.

Of equal importance was the absence of cohesion in the party itself. This arose in part from the democratic traditions of the labour movement, which were by no means adjusted to the exigencies of parliamentary life. The Labour Party was in any case, as we have seen, a federation of independent organisations, and it was natural that the differences existing among the bodies sponsoring the M.P.s, and particularly those between the Socialist societies and the trade unions, should appear on the parliamentary scene. The difficulties were exemplified by almost the first act of the parliamentary party — the election of a chairman (he was not known, as in the case of the other parties, as a leader). There were two candidates : Hardie of the I.L.P., who was the Socialist candidate, and Shackleton of the Cotton Weavers, who was a non-Socialist trade union leader. On the first vote, which was an open one, the two men obtained equal support, Ramsay MacDonald as secretary of the extra-parliamentary party abstaining. Then, a ballot was held : MacDonald again abstained and the result was the same. Finally, a second ballot took place with MacDonald participating and Hardie was elected. The result of this division was that Hardie had to undertake not to make his chairmanship a permanent one, but to encourage a rotation of the office. Consequently he was succeeded in 1908 by Henderson who, as the Socialists put it, was one of the 'old gang' of trade-union leaders ; and in 1910 Henderson was succeeded by George Barnes, the secretary of the Engineers. Barnes fell ill in 1911 and his place was then taken by MacDonald, whose parliamentary ability fully matched his administrative talents.

With the chairmanship changing hands so frequently,

and with major differences in any case existing in the political standpoint of the members of the party, it was inevitable that discipline was weak. Hardie himself proved to be an indifferent parliamentarian, rather inclined to play the lone wolf, and by no means ready to adapt himself to collective decisions. When at the 1907 Labour Party conference a resolution was passed opposing any women's suffrage legislation on a property franchise, Hardie at once said that he would resign from the parliamentary party rather than accept this as his policy. The parliamentary party therefore hastily passed a resolution allowing him to vote on this issue contrary to party policy.[1] In later years, this formed a valuable precedent for others who wished to express their own disagreements with the collective will: it was, in fact, the origin of the well-known 'conscience clause' which was embodied in the party's Standing Orders.

Hardie as chairman constantly left it to Henderson, the party whip, to negotiate 'behind the Speaker's chair' about the conduct of business; and in 1907 for a large part of the session he was away ill. When in 1908 Henderson became chairman, therefore, he was not without experience. But Hardie regarded him with grave suspicion as being little more than a Liberal. Hardie wrote a revealing letter to his I.L.P. colleague Bruce Glasier at the end of Henderson's first year of office:

> I suppose we are in for another year of Henderson's chairmanship, which means that reaction and timidity will be in the ascendancy with disastrous effects to our side of the movement in the country. I grow weary of apologising for a state of things for which I am not responsible and with which I have scant sympathy. Then when the miners come in the Annual Conferences will be controlled by Coal and Cotton, and . . . that means more reaction. There are times when I confess to feeling sore at seeing the fruits of our years of toil being garnered by men who were never of us, and who even now would trick us out . . .[2]

This sort of mutual suspicion and disagreement resulted

in open conflicts on many issues, and after 1910 a distinct 'cave' of Socialist rebels, consisting of Hardie, Snowden and Lansbury, made its appearance. MacDonald did not join them, and when he became chairman of the party he ran into just as much difficulty as Henderson had encountered with the Socialist rebels. As W. J. Braithwaite, the Treasury official helping to prepare the Insurance Act, said of the officials of the Labour Party in 1911 : 'They don't speak for their men, don't know what their men want, and can't bind their men to obey — rather difficult people to deal with.'[3]

(2)

If the Socialists inside the parliamentary party were restive and embittered with their trade-unionist colleagues, it goes without saying that the extra-parliamentary Socialists were even more restive and bitter. The rank and file of the I.L.P. resented the limitations on their activity that were imposed by their leaders' association with the Labour Party, and through the Labour Party, with the Liberals. The Trades Disputes Act (restoring the *status quo ante* Taff Vale) and the very limited Provision of School Meals Act — the two Labour successes of 1906 — cut very little ice with the Socialists. Their frustration found a striking expression as early as 1907, when a young I.L.P.er called Victor Grayson was put up as a candidate at a by-election in the Colne Valley. Grayson went about his adoption incorrectly and failed to get endorsement from the local union leaders. He consequently had to fight without the official support of the Labour Party. But he made a virtue of this necessity, and proclaiming himself a 'clean Socialist' he managed to win a former Liberal seat in a three-cornered contest. The result was startling to all the political parties, and embarrassing to the Labour Party. It may well be that it was this apparent 'boom' in Socialism which convinced Lloyd George of the need to press for social reform inside the Cabinet.

Grayson, at Westminster, was regarded as a pariah by

the Labour M.P.s. This was to a large extent his own
fault, for he was anxious to make a sensation at Westminster
rather than to seek allies with whom he might co-operate
for constructive purposes. Keir Hardie, who had practised
somewhat similar tactics in the 1890's, resented their continuation in a period when a Labour Party already existed.
His resentment, however, would have been more justifiable
if the Labour Party had in fact been winning attention for
a constructive programme: yet as Hardie himself admitted
this was not the case — indeed, he declared in 1910 that
the Labour Party had 'almost ceased to count'.[4]

Part of the trouble, of course, lay in the fact that the
Liberal Party under pressure from Lloyd George was taking
the initiative from 1908 onwards. We still do not know
how far Lloyd George as Chancellor of the Exchequer deliberately provoked the rejection of his budget by the House
of Lords; but he must have realised at an early stage that
such a development was of much value to the Liberals, for
it gave them a constitutional issue on which to go to the
country — an issue that would unite their variegated supporters, who were still inclined to disagree about social
reform, and at the same time an issue on which the Labour
Party had nothing distinctive to propose. In fact, the
reforms proposed in the 1909 budget — a tax on land values
and a small supertax being the main novelties — were not
particularly startling, but rather irritating; and the Unionist
majority in the Lords undoubtedly committed a serious
tactical error in rejecting the budget, thereby putting themselves on dangerous constitutional ground.

With an election pending in 1909, the Labour Party
was suddenly struck an unexpected blow in the law-courts.
This was the Osborne Judgment, which declared its system
of fund-raising from the trade unions to be illegal. Osborne
was a member of the Amalgamated Society of Railway
Servants who objected to paying a compulsory levy for the
upkeep of the Labour M.P.s. He sought an injunction
against the union, and this was upheld by the courts and
on appeal by the House of Lords. The view taken by the

Lords was that, since political action was not mentioned among the legitimate objects of unions in the Trade Union Act of 1876, it was therefore illegal. The Lords also commented unfavourably upon the system whereby Labour M.P.s were obliged to give a pledge to abide by the party's instructions in their behaviour in the House of Commons.

This decision crippled the party financially, and various attempts made by the unions to continue their support for the Labour Party on a voluntary basis collapsed in the face of the apathy of their members. The party with the support of the T.U.C. determined to secure legislation to reverse the decision. In the meantime, it had to fight the two general elections of 1910, and in both its dependence upon the Liberals was very obvious. In the January election, not a single member was returned against official Liberal opposition; the same was true of the December election except for two mining seats.

In the earlier of these general elections Grayson was defeated. But he had already become of more significance outside Parliament than in it, for he was running a vigorous campaign to free the Socialist movement of the encumbrance of the 'Labour alliance', as he saw it. This campaign won support, not only from the dogmatically Marxist S.D.F. (as was to be expected), but also from a large proportion of the rank and file of the I.L.P. Ever since 1907 I.L.P. conferences had become a real test of strength for Keir Hardie and Ramsay MacDonald, and in 1909, after an unfavourable vote, Hardie, MacDonald, Snowden, and Bruce Glasier, the 'big four' of the I.L.P., all resigned from the Council of the organisation, although their policy was in the end endorsed.

In 1910 the campaign inside the I.L.P. went a stage further when four of the new members of the Council published a pamphlet entitled *Let Us Reform the Labour Party*. Known as the 'Green Manifesto' because of the colour of its cover, it fiercely denounced the leadership for abandoning the original position of the I.L.P., which, it said, was

Keir Hardie (1856-1915)

Ramsay MacDonald (1866-1937)

that 'Labour must fight for Socialism and its own hand against BOTH the Capitalist parties IMPARTIALLY'.[5] The contest inside the I.L.P. became more embittered, but the rebels failed to win control of the party, perhaps because Grayson was not a good leader — he had taken heavily to drink, and was very unreliable about attending meetings.

In 1911 the opponents of the 'Labour alliance', both inside and outside the I.L.P., decided to found a new united Socialist organisation. This took the name of British Socialist Party (B.S.P.). The largest element in its composition was the S.D.F., whose veteran leader, H. M. Hyndman, became chairman of the new body. But it also included many individual rebels and even whole branches from the I.L.P., as well as other Socialists such as those belonging to the Clarion Fellowship, which was sponsored by Robert Blatchford's *Clarion* newspaper. At the end of its first year of activity the B.S.P. claimed a membership of some 15,000 — half the size of the I.L.P. at its peak. Thereafter, the B.S.P. membership dwindled until at the outbreak of war in 1914 it seemed to contain few more than had been in the old S.D.F. By this time, furthermore, it was seeking reaffiliation to the Labour Party.

The assault of the discontented Socialists upon the alliance of the I.L.P. with the trade unionists was thus but narrowly defeated in 1909–11, but for various reasons — mainly the emergence of new issues — it weakened thereafter. In the course of 1911 a new challenge to the Labour Party appeared among its own affiliated organisations. This was a challenge inside the unions, and it arose from the Syndicalist movement, which sought to dispense with politics, or at least parliamentary politics, altogether. The object of Syndicalism was to win control of the economy by industrial action, and as a first step it sought to turn the unions into agents of its purpose, making them industrial unions instead of craft unions, and effecting amalgamations of small societies in the same or kindred industries. The most prominent Syndicalist leader was Tom Mann, who had come to public notice for his part in the 1889 dock strike, but who since then for ten years or so had been working in New Zealand and Australia. Mann now reinforced his renown by successfully conducting a large-scale transport strike on Merseyside. The Syndicalist movement absorbed the energies of a good many of the more militant Socialists, and it consequently had a weakening effect on the B.S.P., but it did not make very much permanent impression upon the officialdom of the unions. Its greatest success was perhaps in the field of amalgamation, and in particular it led to the merging of the Railway Servants and two other railwaymen's unions into the National Union of Railwaymen. But its limited success even among railwaymen is shown by the continued existence of two other unions in the industry, the Locomotive Engineers and Firemen and the Railway Clerks. Nevertheless, a younger generation of trade unionists was much influenced by Syndicalism, perhaps especially the miners, who in these years as the price of coal went down, and with it, their wages, grew more and more impatient with their generally conservative leaders.

A further result of Syndicalism was that an interesting daily labour newspaper called the *Herald* came into existence. It was largely in the hands of George Lansbury, who was a left-wing Socialist owing a nominal allegiance to the I.L.P. Its contributors were all rebels of one sort or another, but not necessarily Syndicalists or even Socialists. They included many able men, for instance, G. K. Chesterton, Hilaire Belloc, the cartoonist Will Dyson, and the young Oxford don G. D. H. Cole, who evolved the idea of Guild Socialism as a sort of compromise between parliamentary action and the popular desire for workers' control of industry. The *Herald*, though perpetually in danger of financial collapse, was much more interesting than the official Labour newspaper, the *Daily Citizen*, which, sponsored by the Labour Party and the T.U.C., came into existence in 1912. It was significant that when war broke out in 1914 the *Daily Citizen* expired immediately, while the *Herald* managed to struggle on and to survive for a more important role in the post-war world.

(3)

As has been said, the most difficult time for the Labour Party was after the 1910 elections, when it had to sustain the Liberal Party in power at all costs, and at the same time seek from it the concession of legislation to reverse the Osborne Judgment. But the Liberals had their own programme of legislation, and all that the Labour Party could obtain in 1911 was the introduction of state payment of M.P.s, in return for which MacDonald gave Lloyd George a guarantee that the party would support his Insurance Bill.[6] The state payment of members was of advantage to the Labour Party in easing the financial problem facing its M.P.s, but it obviously weakened the discipline of the parliamentary party still further, particularly as it was felt desirable to abandon the practice introduced in 1903 of requiring the M.P.s or candidates to sign a pledge to observe the party's constitution and Standing Orders.

MacDonald himself, so far as one can tell, sincerely believed in the principles of Lloyd George's Insurance Act, and not least in the contributory principle, which many Socialists felt to be contrary to their faith. As he said in his Second Reading speech, 'I am in favour of insurance and not of free gift'.[7] On the other hand, Snowden and the Webbs, together with Lansbury who had served with Mrs. Webb on the Poor Law Commission, were united in opposition to this view. Their aim was a National Health Service undertaking preventive measures for the benefit of the whole community. The difficulty with this distinctly more Socialist view was the cost, which would be difficult to control, unlike the actuarially sound insurance scheme that Lloyd George introduced. Lloyd George's scheme, however, proved preferable to the trade unionists, once they understood that the unions would be approved societies for the purpose of the Act. The upshot was that most of the Labour Party supported the government in the lobbies on this question, and there was only a small minority of irreconcilable Socialists who joined the irreconcilable Tories in opposition to it.

In 1913 the unhappy position of Labour Party finances was cleared up by the passing of the Trade Union Act. Under the Act, trade unions were permitted to raise contributions from their members for political purposes, provided that they kept their political fund separate from their funds for industrial and general purposes. Union members were to be allowed to contract out of paying the contributions for political purposes if they desired to do so, simply by making a written statement of their intention. Opponents of the Labour Party in the Commons did not like this arrangement, as they felt that union members would be subject to intimidation to prevent them from contracting out. They suggested instead that union members should be regarded as non-contributors to the political fund unless they actually contracted in. But the latter view naturally did not commend itself to the Labour leaders in view of their recent experience with voluntary funds, and the bill went through in the form that they were prepared to accept.

By this time the government was finding, amidst all its other distractions, including the great struggle over Irish Home Rule, that an ever greater proportion of the budget had to be devoted to armaments, particularly for a naval building programme to keep well ahead of the German effort. The majority of Labour M.P.s, together with a substantial minority of Liberals, favoured resistance to this tendency. For ideological reasons, they were quite as suspicious of Russia as of Germany, and they held that the best thing for Britain to do was to keep out of continental quarrels by a policy of isolation. Many of them regarded military expenditure as an unwelcome diversion of funds which might otherwise be spent on social reform.

The Socialists were also inclined to oppose armaments because of their faith in the Socialist International, in which the German party was the largest single element. Successive congresses of the International had pledged the parties in the various countries to agitate against war, and Keir Hardie in 1910 attempted to secure the acceptance of a proposal for an international general strike in the event of hostilities. Although this proposal was rejected by the congress largely at the instance of the Germans who could see that it would prove impracticable, many Socialists retained a vague belief that somehow or other the International would be able to play a part in the prevention of a major war.

Inside the Labour Party, the discussion of foreign affairs was usually left to the Socialists : the trade-union members rarely worried their heads about it. But when it came to voting against the naval and military estimates, there were some who did not follow the majority of the party. The naval estimates, for instance, were supported by Labour M.P.s representing dockyard constituencies, as they did not want to be accused of depriving their constituents of much-needed employment. As a Conservative M.P. rather unkindly pointed out, 'I have noticed when members of the Labour Party happen to represent a dockyard constituency or a district in which armaments are created that there are no greater jingoes in the House'.[8] In addition, Will Thorne, who was a member of the S.D.F., believed like the other members of that organisation in a form of conscription known as 'the citizen army', which was based on the idea that a revolution could best be effected when all members of the working class had some training in the use of arms.

In general, however, the realities of Britain's diplomatic and military commitments made little impact upon the Labour Party. Nor was the party very much to blame for this : fearful of hostile reaction among their own supporters, Asquith and Grey took care not to reveal the nature of the military and naval agreements made with France. The result was an absence of informed discussion on one of the most vital topics of the day. Under the circumstances, it can be readily understood how it was that the Labour Party failed to come to grips with the real issues involved.

(4)

There is no doubt that many of the difficulties of the party in this period derived from its close association with the Liberals in the 1906 election. Although the electoral agreement had paid immediate dividends, there were long-term liabilities for the Labour Party which perhaps only Herbert Gladstone had fully appreciated. A party which had set out to represent a whole social class had become identified with the sectional interests of Liberalism — with Free Trade, Nonconformity, and Home Rule. The accession of the miners' M.P.s in 1909 only increased the tendency, for the miners' leaders of this period were much less militant than the leaders of other unions. The necessity of supporting the Liberal Government during the difficult years when the Osborne Judgment was in operation completed the subordination of the Parliamentary Labour Party to the position of 'handmaiden of Liberalism'.

Yet the parliamentary party was only part of a larger whole — the labour movement. The future of the parliamentary party lay to a very large extent with the trade unions and Socialist societies and perhaps even more with the local L.R.C.s or Labour Parties that began to grow up in the constituencies. A comparison of the official figures of membership of the party in 1906 and 1914 shows that considerable growth had taken place in all these categories. In 1914 the trade-union membership had fallen back as a result of the Osborne Judgment, but it was still over $1\frac{1}{2}$ million, whereas in 1906 it had been only about 900,000. The affiliated membership of the Socialist societies — that is, the I.L.P. and the very much smaller Fabian Society — had grown from less than 17,000 to about 33,000 ; and the B.S.P. was applying to rejoin. Even more striking, however, was the growth of the party's local organisations. By 1915, no less than eighty-five trades councils were affiliated, and there were also some seventy-three local Labour Parties. There was some overlapping of political function between local Labour Parties and trades councils, and in a few towns both were recorded as being affiliated to the national Labour Party. But in 1906 there had been only eighty-three of both types of organisation put together. These organisations, which in most cases secured affiliations both from local trade-union branches and from local branches of the Socialist societies, were especially important for strengthening the party's hold in the constituencies.

In other ways, too, the party was constantly developing its strength. It had a national agent and two full-time party agents for visiting the constituencies; it also paid subsidies towards the maintenance of twenty local agents. Moreover, the party's influence gradually extended into areas which in 1906 had been almost untouched. In Scotland, for instance, where a quite separate but very weak body called the Scottish Workers Representation Committee had existed, responsibility had been assumed by a Scottish Council of the Labour Party, which was much more successful. In addition, a London Labour Party for the metropolitan area was belatedly established in 1914 — a development that had been delayed by the grip of the S.D.F. and then the B.S.P. upon the London Trades Council, and the unwillingness of that body up till 1914 to regard the Labour Party with favour. There were, of course, already a number of local Labour Parties in London boroughs or constituencies. Municipal activity by local parties and trades councils was constantly expanding, though London was late in the movement, owing to the strength of the old Progressive alliance on the L.C.C. But the defeat of the Progressives in 1907, and the outside propaganda work of the Labour M.P.s when they were resident in London, enabled a Labour group to develop on the L.C.C. from 1910 onwards.

The increasing size of the extra-parliamentary party meant that one man could no longer effectively combine the secretaryship with major parliamentary duties. Ramsay MacDonald from 1906 to 1911 managed to be secretary of both the parliamentary and the extra-parliamentary party; but by 1910 he was an obvious candidate for the chairmanship of the parliamentary party and it was clear that he could not do justice both to this post and to his extra-parliamentary responsibilities. He seems to have genuinely wanted the chairmanship, because of a feeling that he alone could provide the necessary leadership (and leadership, of course, was something rather more than earlier chairmen had provided). In 1910 he wrote to Hardie: 'I do not care a dump about the chairmanship, but I do want the party to be led. . . . Let it be led to the devil if you like, but do not let it be the nerveless thing of the past session'.[9] The illness of George Barnes enabled him to take over the chairmanship at the beginning of 1911, and the following year he relinquished the secretaryship of the external organisation to Arthur Henderson.

Arthur Henderson, as a non-Socialist ex-Liberal, had always been rather suspect among the Socialists of the Labour Party. But he had developed a considerable degree of loyalty to the organisation, and as a former official of an old craft union — the Friendly Society of Ironfounders — he carried great influence with the union element in the party. As secretary of the party, he now decided to become a Socialist, which he did by joining the Fabian Society. How far this was a matter of conviction is perhaps doubtful; there were, in fact, organisational reasons for his action. MacDonald, as secretary of the Labour Party, was also secretary of the British Bureau of the Socialist International. If Henderson were not nominally a Socialist he could not take this post, and therefore a key position in the International would probably fall to the Marxist B.S.P. To prevent this happening, Henderson underwent a new political baptism, if not a conversion.

Hardie was now ageing rapidly and it became obvious that the two most important figures in the party were MacDonald and Henderson. MacDonald was successful in his aim of turning the chairmanship of the parliamentary party into an effective leadership (the use of the word 'leader', however, was still not accepted); but inevitably he lost his close links with the organisation in the constituencies. A certain testiness and insensitivity to criticism also made him many enemies. Henderson, on the other hand, rapidly matured in experience and gained great popularity. But there was little conflict between the two men. Henderson was content to regard MacDonald as by far the most suitable parliamentary spokesman, for he had a high regard for his abilities. Their co-operation provided the party with an effective working team, and this accounts for the re-election of MacDonald as chairman of the parliamentary party in each successive session from 1911 to the outbreak of war.

By 1914, then, the Labour Party was consolidating its influence in towns and industrial areas throughout Britain. It had little or no support in purely agricultural constituencies, but it was getting into a position from which it might be able to contest a much increased range of constituencies, instead of the mere fifty of 1906. In the first 1910 election it had seventy-eight candidates; in the second 1910 election, for obvious reasons, it dropped back to fifty-six. But it was equally obvious that at an election in 1914 or 1915 it would be able to contest a hundred or more seats. The 1903 agreement with the Liberals would then become a thing of the past. Much uncertainty remained, however, owing to the failure to solve the problem of Irish Home Rule. The Labour Party had been obliged to support the Liberals on this issue, but in the course of 1914 it looked as if the struggle would end only in civil war.

Suddenly, however, the political pattern was transformed by an external catalyst — that of war on the continent of Europe, in which Britain quickly became involved.

NOTES

1. At their meeting on 11 Feb. 1907. See *Labour Party Quarterly Circular*, Apr. 1907, p. 3.
2. Hardie to Glasier, 27 Dec. 1908, Glasier Papers.
3. W. J. Braithwaite, diary 28 July, 1911, quoted in his *Lloyd George's Ambulance Wagon* (1957), p. 196.

4. I.L.P. *Annual Report* (1910), p. 58.
5. Leonard Hall *et al.*, *Let Us Reform the Labour Party* (1910), p. 3.
6. MacDonald to Master of Elibank, 4 Oct. 1911, quoted Frank Owen, *Tempestuous Journey* (1954), pp. 207 f.
7. Hansard, *Parliamentary Debates*, ser. 5, xxvi, 725.
8. Quoted W. P. Maddox, *Foreign Relations in British Labour Politics* (Cambridge, Mass., 1934), p. 209.
9. MacDonald to Hardie, 1 Feb. 1910, Hardie Papers.

FURTHER READING

Documented narratives of Labour Party history covering this and later periods are to be found in Carl F. Brand, *The British Labour Party: A Short History* (Stanford, Calif., 1965), and R. Miliband, *Parliamentary Socialism* (1961), which has a strong left-wing bias. But one most valuable contribution to the study of the party in 1906–14 is Clegg, Fox and Thompson, *op. cit.* (see p. 17), though its narrative ends in 1910. Here, the records of the Joint Board have been drawn upon to show that friction developed when Shackleton, as chairman of the Parliamentary Committee of the T.U.C., discussed details of legislation with Liberal ministers without consulting Hardie or Henderson, the Labour Party's chairmen. From 1910 onwards, an equally valuable study of party organisation, based on the papers at Transport House, is R. McKibbin, *Evolution of the Labour Party, 1910–1924* (Oxford, 1974).

The book by W. P. Maddox, cited above, provides valuable analysis of policy formation within the party. The biographies *Keir Hardie* by Morgan and *Ramsay MacDonald* by Marquand (see p. 16) are again of value. For the impact of the law see Henry Pelling, 'The Politics of the Osborne Judgment', *Historical Journal*, 25 (1982). For the S.D.F. and B.S.P. see C. Tsuzuki, *H. M. Hyndman and British Socialism* (1961); for Fabianism, see A. M. MacBriar, *Fabian Socialism and English Politics, 1884–1918* (Cambridge, 1962). K. D. Brown, *The First Labour Party, 1906–1914* (1985) contains interesting essays on aspects of party development in the period. See also D. J. Newton, *British Labour, European Socialism and the Struggle for Peace, 1889–1914* (Oxford, 1985).

CHAPTER III

Henderson's Party : War and Reconstruction
(*1914–22*)

(1)

ALTHOUGH the Labour Party had by no means ignored questions of foreign policy before July 1914, it was only with the outbreak of war that they became of paramount importance. From then onwards until 1918 and indeed in the early post-war years, up to 1922, issues of war and diplomacy were dominant in the party's councils.

As the Sarajevo crisis reached its climax at the end of July, the Labour Party took a vigorous share in the agitation against war which was sponsored throughout Europe by the Socialist International. On Sunday 1st August Germany declared war on Russia ; and next day Keir Hardie and Arthur Henderson took part in a mass demonstration in Trafalgar Square, urging the government to keep out. On Monday 3rd August Germany declared war on France ; and that morning the Parliamentary Labour Party met and decided to oppose British intervention when the Commons debated the question in the afternoon. Consequently, although Sir Edward Grey made an impassioned appeal for aid to France, and although he was supported not only by the Conservatives but also by the Irish Nationalists, Ramsay MacDonald sounded a discordant note by registering his party's disapproval. MacDonald's speech, significantly enough, was in large part an appeal to the rank and file of the Liberal Party. 'Whatever may happen,' he declared,

whatever may be said about us, we will take the action . . . of saying that this country ought to have remained neutral, because in the deepest parts of our hearts we believe that that was right and that that alone was consistent with the honour of our country and the traditions of the Party that are now in office.[1]

But Grey's speech and, more particularly, the invasion of Belgium which took place next day (4th August) had the effect of transforming public opinion. It now became clear that there was almost universal enthusiasm for the declaration of war, and many of those who had previously hesitated were convinced by the need to fight on behalf of Belgium, whether for the sake of honour or for reasons of national expediency. The British ultimatum to Germany expired late in the evening of 4th August; and next morning, when the National Executive of the Labour Party met, it was apparent that the party no longer presented a united front of opposition to the war. The resolution that it passed, and which was then endorsed at a joint meeting with the parliamentary party, was clearly a compromise. It deplored the fact that British support had been committed to France 'without the knowledge of our people', but it did not express direct opposition to the war, merely saying that it was the duty of the labour movement to 'secure peace at the earliest possible moment on such conditions as will provide the best opportunities for the re-establishment of amicable feelings between the workers of Europe'.[2] The vagueness of this statement shows that it was designed to hide serious differences. The fact was that only the I.L.P. leaders were advocating a downright opposition to the war, on the lines of their campaign against the South African War. The majority of Labour M.P.s felt that they must support the war effort now that hostilities had begun. They were encouraged in this view by the break-up of the façade of unity among continental Socialists, as the French and Belgian leaders called for resistance to the German invaders, and the German Social-Democratic M.P.s voted war credits for the Kaiser's armies.

Under these circumstances, Ramsay MacDonald found

it necessary to resign the leadership of the parliamentary party. The actual issue was the party's attitude to the supplementary estimates moved by the Prime Minister on 6th August, notice of which was given the previous day. At a meeting late on the 5th, the party decided not to oppose these estimates, and MacDonald thereupon resigned. Arthur Henderson was appointed to take his place, and soon the great majority of the Labour Party under Henderson's lead was supporting the government, taking part in a recruiting campaign and accepting an electoral truce for the duration of the war. MacDonald and most of his I.L.P. colleagues found themselves fighting a lonely battle against the war with the help of a small minority of Liberals. For propaganda against the war, MacDonald joined with four anti-war Liberals, Norman Angell, E. D. Morel, Charles Trevelyan, and Arthur Ponsonby, to form in September 1914 a body called the Union of Democratic Control. The U.D.C. demanded democratic control of foreign policy, no annexations, an international organisation to maintain peace, and disarmament. New alignments thus cut across the ranks of the Labour Party, and threatened its continued existence as a political force.

Yet at the time, there were few who thought that the war would last as long as a year. Although Henderson had disagreed with MacDonald and had taken his place as party chairman, he did not want to expel the anti-war minority from membership of the party, for he expected an early return to the peace-time condition of politics. The analogy of the Liberal Party's toleration of internal disagreements during the South African War, and its speedy recovery of unity and rise to power afterwards, must have been present in many minds. Furthermore, MacDonald and Henderson at least could still agree in condemning Grey's conduct of pre-war diplomacy; and it was significant that Henderson became a member, albeit an inactive member, of the U.D.C. In practice it proved possible for all sections of the labour movement to collaborate in seeking measures to safeguard living standards in the changed circumstances of war. As early as 5th August a War Emergency Workers' National Committee had been set up at a joint conference of labour and socialist organisations which had been summoned by Arthur Henderson in his capacity as Secretary of the Labour Party. The Workers' National Committee included both supporters and opponents of the war, for they found plenty of common ground on such issues as war-time unemployment, inflation, and profiteering.

As the war dragged on into 1915, however, collaboration between the different sections of the movement was subjected to increasing strain. In May 1915 Arthur Henderson was invited to join the First Coalition under Asquith. He referred the matter to the parliamentary party, which by a tiny majority was opposed to taking office; but the National Executive favoured it, and the issue was resolved by a joint meeting of the Executive and the parliamentary party, at which the majority of the latter were overruled. The difference of attitude of the two bodies may be explained by the greater strength of the I.L.P. in Parliament. Henderson then became President of the Board of Education, a somewhat unsuitable post, but with a seat in the Cabinet; and two other Labour M.P.s took junior office.

The influence of the Labour Party upon the actual conduct of government was not very noticeable at first. It seemed rather that the party was a prisoner of the other parties, obliged to take responsibility for various measures that were bound to be unpopular in the labour movement. One highly controversial issue was the dilution of labour in the factories — that is, the admission of unskilled workers into occupations hitherto reserved for craftsmen who had served their apprenticeship. Another was military conscription, which was strongly opposed by most sections of the labour movement. Members of the government soon began to realise that the participation of Henderson and his colleagues in office did not guarantee the loyalty of all the workers in the factories and mines. There was much industrial unrest, particularly on Clydeside; and early in 1916, when the conscription bill was being debated, the annual conference of the Labour Party went on record as opposed to the principle, although it coupled this with an indication that the party would cease to agitate the question if the bill was passed.

Lloyd George as Minister of Munitions had had direct experience of the importance of conciliating labour; and when in December 1916 he formed a government to replace that of Asquith he found it convenient to offer the Labour Party considerably better terms than before for its participation in the government. In fact, he gave an interview to 'a very representative attendance of both the Executive and the Parliamentary Party', at which he gave various undertakings about his policy and the part that he would enable Labour to play in the government. He promised state control of the mines and of shipping, and the introduction of an effective system of food rationing. This offer was too good to refuse; and so members of the Labour Party were authorised to enter the government again. Henderson this time was in a small War Cabinet of five members, and two other Labour M.P.s, John Hodge and George Barnes, became Minister of Labour and Minister of Pensions respectively, both of these ministries being new creations. Several other Labour M.P.s were appointed to junior posts.

At the beginning of 1917, therefore, there seemed to be a particularly deep cleavage between the Labour Party majority, which was so fully committed to Lloyd George's 'Win the War' government, and the I.L.P. minority, many of whose younger members were resisting the call-up and being taken away to military detention. It was significant that at the annual conference of the Labour Party in January a move was made to exclude the influence of the Socialist societies from the National Executive. It was proposed by union representatives, and carried by a narrow majority against the advice of Henderson, that the Executive members should all be elected by vote of the whole conference. This decision broke up the existing federal structure of the party, whereby both the Socialist societies and the trade unions elected their separate representatives; and it inevitably meant trade-union nomination of the entire body. The I.L.P. leaders naturally found it particularly obnoxious, and they began to talk of leaving the party. 'I am not going to sneak about', wrote MacDonald,

> and bargain for Trade Union votes for I.L.P. candidates for the Executive. . . . If a split were to come owing to the oppressive use of the block vote of some of the larger unions, I would do what I could to form a new Labour combination for political purposes.[3]

As it happened, however, — or was this Henderson's deliberate stage-management? — the proposal had only come up after the election of the Executive members for the following year; and by 1918, as we shall see, the political situation had entirely changed, so that the use of the block vote became far from 'oppressive', at least in the sense that MacDonald wished to imply.

(2)

The main changes that took place in the political climate in 1917 were due to the two revolutions in Russia and to the entry of the United States into the war. The first Russian Revolution was greeted with great enthusiasm on the Left, as was shown by the success of a special conference at Leeds in June, summoned by the United Socialist Council. This body was an unofficial body so far as the Labour Party was concerned, but it was really the joint voice of the I.L.P. and the B.S.P., which were both now affiliated to the Labour Party. The conference was attended by over a thousand delegates from local Socialist branches, from trade-union branches, and from trades councils. It expressed great gratification at the overthrow of Tsarism and saluted the prospect of a peace without annexations. It even urged the establishment of Soldiers' and Workmen's Councils in Britain, on the Russian model, but this was really more a gesture of sympathy for the Russians than a carefully prepared move in the direction of a British revolution : it had almost no practical consequences.

What was significant, however, was the change of attitude of the trade-union rank and file, which was also reflected in the official leadership of the Labour Party itself. At the suggestion of Lloyd George, who wanted to keep Russia in the war, Henderson was sent to visit Russia ; and on his return he announced himself of the opinion that the best way to keep the Russians in line with the Western Allies was to explore in conjunction with them the basis for a negotiated peace.

Henderson also favoured the despatch of delegates from Britain to a proposed International Socialist Congress at Stockholm, which it was expected that German Socialists would attend. Further, he persuaded a special conference of the Labour Party to agree with him. This, however, precipitated a crisis with his colleagues in the War Cabinet. Summoned to a meeting of this body, of which he had been a member since the government was formed, Henderson was kept outside the door while its other members discussed his position. He was then formally rebuked by Lloyd George and accordingly resigned in a state of great indignation. It was obvious that Lloyd George, who had originally been sympathetic to Henderson's views on relations with Russia, had had his hand forced by the other members of the Cabinet. The crisis, later known as the 'doormat incident', was not revealed to the public until a fortnight later ; and Lloyd George managed to soften its impact by at once replacing Henderson with another Labour Party member, George Barnes, and by bringing another Labour M.P., George Wardle, into the government. The affair was thus kept on a personal level between Henderson and the Prime Minister ; and the government retained the support of the Labour Party while refusing exit visas for the Stockholm Conference.

All the same, the 'doormat incident' proved to be a turning-point in the history of the Labour Party. From that time onwards, Henderson, who was still secretary of the party, began to devote himself largely to its affairs, not only shaping a major reorganisation of its structure, but also devising an alternative foreign policy to that of the government. Henderson's work thus prepared the party to undertake the responsibilities of leading the opposition in the event of a general election. The opportunity was obvious, owing to the completely divided state of the Liberal Party. Even Walter Hines Page, the American ambassador, who was no friend to labour, could see the implications of Henderson's policy: as he wrote to President Wilson in January 1918, 'The Labour Party is already playing for supremacy'. Henderson, unlike MacDonald, was quite willing to pick the brains of the intellectuals; and by December 1917 Beatrice Webb could say that her husband Sidney, who was on the National Executive as the representative of the Fabian Society, had become 'the intellectual leader of the Labour Party'.[4]

The most important change, however, was in the attitude of both the leadership and the rank and file of the trade unions. Already before the war it was the Miners Federation and the Railwaymen which had become the most radical of the unions, and these organisations, led by Robert Smillie and J. H. Thomas respectively, now began to press for a more independent political policy both by the T.U.C. and by the Labour Party. In 1917 the Parliamentary Committee of the T.U.C., realising both its power and its opportunity, began to take an active part in shaping a new foreign policy — a decision that was welcomed by Henderson. Consequently, when Henderson, with the help of Sidney Webb and Ramsay MacDonald, drew up a 'Memorandum on War Aims' towards the end of 1917, they secured its approval by both the National Executive of the party and the Parliamentary Committee of the T.U.C. The Memorandum demanded the establishment of a League of Nations and of machinery for the mediation of international disputes; international trusteeship of African colonies; and international action to deal with economic problems such as the supply of raw materials.

These far-sighted recommendations alienated some extreme 'patriotic' union leaders, some of whom seceded from the party. But they won such an overwhelming endorsement from the unions as a whole that they had much influence in the world, both upon Lloyd George and upon President Wilson, who through various agents kept a close watch on the development of British opinion. Lloyd George soon afterwards made a statement on war aims to a conference of trade unionists, and although it was in studiously vague terms it seemed to show some Labour Party influence ; and President Wilson's Fourteen Points, which were enunciated a few days later, followed the same lines.

Meanwhile Henderson with the aid of Sidney Webb had also been preparing a new draft constitution for the Labour Party. His object was to weld the Socialist and trade-union elements firmly together and to provide for the admission to full membership of people who were not trade unionists : middle-class people, for instance, and also women, who were shortly to get the vote. The new draft therefore arranged for the opening of the local Labour Parties to individual membership, so that it would no longer be necessary for the Labour Party supporter to secure his membership of the party through one of the affiliated Socialist societies or trade unions. The composition of the Executive was to be changed : out of a proposed total of twenty-one seats, no less than five were to be reserved for nominees of local Labour Parties and another four for women. The remaining seats would be available for the nominees of trade unions and Socialist societies, between whom no distinction now remained. In accordance with the resolution of the 1917 conference, the actual election to all seats on the Executive was to be done by the whole conference : the federal principle had thus been abandoned.

If the Executive was henceforth to be completely dominated by the union block vote, at least the Socialists were to gain by the party's adoption of a Socialist constitution. This was drafted by Sidney Webb, who produced the celebrated Clause Four of the 'Party Objects' which for the first time explicitly committed the party to a Socialist basis :

> To secure for the producers by hand and brain the full fruits of their industry, and the most equitable distribution thereof that may be possible, upon the basis of the common ownership of the means of production and the best obtainable system of popular administration and control of each industry or service.[5]

It was a striking demonstration of the leftward trend in the unions that this constitution was adopted in February 1918 with only one amendment of any importance — the addition of two more seats for the affiliated societies (in effect, for the trade unions), bringing the Executive to a total of twenty-three. Only the I.L.P. really disliked the changes, for it lost its guaranteed seats on the Executive and its influence was rivalled by that of the local Labour Parties.

Only four months later — in June 1918 — the party held another conference, the first under the new constitution. It adopted a policy statement drafted by Sidney Webb, *Labour and the New Social Order*, which was of great importance because it formed the basis of Labour Party policy for over thirty years — in fact, until the general election of 1950. It incorporated four principles, which were set out in the methodical fashion that was typical of the work of Sidney Webb and his wife, Beatrice. The first was the concept of the National Minimum, which the Webbs had advocated at the time of the Poor Law Commission of 1905–9, and which the Labour Party had been slowly working towards before the war. The National Minimum, according to the statement, meant a comprehensive policy of full employment with a minimum wage and a minimum standard of working conditions, together with a maximum working week of forty-eight hours. The second principle was the Democratic Control of Industry : here Webb emphasised the need for nationalisation of industry but also made somewhat vague concessions to the Guild Socialist standpoint which was now so popular among parts of the labour movement — particularly the Miners and the Railwaymen. The third principle was summed up as 'The Revolution in National Finance', which meant in practice the subsidisation of social services by heavy taxation of large incomes and, more specifically, an immediate capital levy to pay off a part of the cost of the war. Finally, the fourth principle was 'The Surplus for the Common Good', which proclaimed that the balance of the nation's wealth should so far as possible be devoted to expanding opportunities in education and in culture for the people as a whole.

The party was thus equipped with a greatly improved constitution, at least for the purpose of making an appeal to the electorate as a whole rather than just to the interest of the unions. It also had a practical programme which in domestic affairs was a compromise between Marxian Socialism on the one hand and the piecemeal social reform of the Chamberlain-Lloyd George type on the other. All this enabled the party to make its bid to rank as an alternative government of the country: a bid that within the first post-war years was to prove unexpectedly successful.

(3)

Meanwhile several members of the Parliamentary Labour Party had remained as members of the Lloyd George Coalition. When the war ended on 11th November, a decision had to be taken on the question of withdrawal from the government. The idea of withdrawal was not welcome to the ministers concerned: Barnes enjoyed being in the War Cabinet and was easily persuaded by Lloyd George of the need for Labour to take part in the post-war settlement; and Clynes, who had become Food Controller, was also happily engaged in administration. Consequently, the Parliamentary Labour Party mostly favoured remaining in office. But the National Executive under Henderson's influence took the opposite view, which was confirmed by a special Labour Party Conference on 14th November.

Clynes reluctantly obeyed the injunction to leave the government; but Barnes and others refused to resign and so forfeited their membership of the Labour Party.

The general election took place in December 1918, and was inevitably a virtual plebiscite for or against Lloyd George, as the architect of victory. In the face of heavy odds, the Labour Party put up a brave fight: it fielded 361 candidates — an enormous increase compared with its previous maximum of 78 in the first 1910 election. The introduction of state payment of returning officers' expenses made by the 1918 Reform Act largely accounted for this increase; but the advantage of this situation was more for the future than for the immediate election, as the tide ran so strongly in favour of the Coalition candidates. In fact, Labour won only fifty-seven seats, which was not a very great improvement on its pre-war totals. It was more significant that in another seventy-nine constituencies where there were three or four candidates, the party ran second to the winner, and ahead of a Liberal. Henceforth, the onus of 'splitting the progressive vote' would lie upon the Liberals. This was especially important now that nearly all the two-member constituencies, which had enabled Liberal and Labour to run in harness, had been abolished by the 1918 Act.

The misfortune of the Parliamentary Labour Party, however, was that for the time being it had lost all its ablest spokesmen. The I.L.P. leaders MacDonald and Snowden were defeated because of their anti-war record; and Arthur Henderson also lost his seat. Of the fifty-seven who found their way to Parliament, twenty-five were miners and twenty-four represented other unions; five were sponsored by local Labour Parties and only three by the I.L.P. Of the well-known leaders of the party, only Clynes survived; and when the parliamentary party met to choose its chairman, it re-elected the Scottish miner Willie Adamson, 'respectable but dull-witted' as Mrs. Webb described him,[6] who had acted as chairman just before the dissolution. It should be added that the Co-operative Union entered politics during the war, and sponsored several candidates, one of whom was elected. The one Co-operative M.P. joined the Parliamentary Labour Party, as did others after later elections; and the 'Co-operative Party' became closely integrated with the Labour Party.

The status of the Parliamentary Labour Party *vis-à-vis* the National Executive and the labour movement at large was now at its nadir. It was bad enough that several of the parliamentary leaders had refused to leave the Coalition Government; it was worse still that the party in the House had lost its remaining members of ability, and that even Henderson, who had so ably conducted the work of re-organisation, had failed to secure re-election. This was just at a moment when the party's revised constitution and policy were beginning to win it an increasing number of middle-class recruits. The demand for a peace without annexations, for instance — the old demand of the U.D.C. — brought to the party many of the able young Liberals who had opposed the war and had then despaired of their own divided party. In more senses than one, they were a 'Foreign Legion' as they were dubbed at the time by one of their own number.[7]

At the same time, it had become obvious that the parliamentary leaders had won their place in the Coalition not because of their numbers in the House but because of the strength of the industrial movement with which they were linked. The readiness of the T.U.C. and of the unions to participate in various types of political action, which became evident for the first time in 1917, remained after the end of the war, and expanded into a threat of direct industrial action for political ends. The most striking example of this was the pressure brought to bear by the T.U.C. in 1920 to secure a termination of British intervention against the Bolsheviks. A Council of Action was set up after the London Dockers, encouraged by their leader Ernest Bevin, had taken the initiative in refusing to load a ship called the *Jolly George* until munitions on board, which were destined for Poland, had been removed. We can now abandon the possibility that this boycott and the threat of further action played a major part in altering Lloyd George's policy and so preventing further British intervention. It was, of course, unconstitutional action which by-passed Parliament and did nothing to enhance the credit of the Parliamentary Labour Party.

The early post-war period was marked by much industrial unrest and trade-union militancy. This was partly because economic conditions were bad — for an immediate post-war boom, coupled with considerable inflation, collapsed suddenly in 1920 into a slump and heavy unemployment. But it was also because the ideas of 'direct action' in vogue just before the war were still widely current among union leaders. In particular, the 'triple alliance' of the Miners, Railwaymen, and Transport Workers, which had been formed just before the war with the object of securing united pressure against their employers, had not yet been put to the test. The idea of a General Strike was also in the air, the miners urging that it would be the best way of securing the nationalisation of the mines which was now their immediate goal.

Unfortunately for the miners, however, even the 'triple alliance' proved unreliable. Like similar alliances in the wider field of international diplomacy, it depended at every test upon the self-interest of each of its components; and in April 1921, on a day known thereafter as 'Black Friday', it broke up when the other unions refused to continue their support for the miners in a strike threat. It came to be recognised that the only way to bring effective joint industrial pressure to bear was to have a unified command of the unions like the General Staff of an army. Consequently, in the course of 1921 the old Parliamentary Committee of the T.U.C., which had been little more than an agency for lobbying the older political parties at Westminster, was transformed into a General Council with greater powers to co-ordinate policy — though not, in the last resort, to order the unions about unless they conceded emergency powers to it. Henceforth the General Council assumed an important political as well as industrial role, building up a headquarters staff which rivalled that of the Labour Party; and it was noteworthy that the ablest union leaders preferred to serve on the General Council rather than to go into what must have seemed the comparative backwater of parliamentary politics. The Labour Party did its best to maintain liaison with the new organisation: for this purpose a National Joint Council was set up, consisting of representatives of the General Council, the Parliamentary Labour Party, and the party's National Executive.

(4)

In the first post-war years, parliamentary politics had little importance for the party as a whole. Although Henderson was returned to the Commons in a by-election in 1919, he did not attempt to resume the chairmanship, preferring to occupy himself in the task of extending extra-parliamentary organisation. In 1920 the obviously incompetent Adamson was succeeded as chairman by Clynes, an abler if not exactly dashing figure. But Henderson held the initiative with his external activities, such as the special Labour Party Commission of Enquiry sent to Ireland to investigate the outrages of the 'Black and Tans'. This did not mean, however, that Henderson had lost interest in parliamentary action; it simply indicated that he was biding his time until a new general election should strengthen the party's representation in the Commons.

The fundamentally constitutional and law-abiding attitude of Henderson and his colleagues was indicated clearly by their reaction to the Communist Party's application for affiliation in 1920. The Communist Party had been formed that year, by the amalgamation of the old B.S.P. and various other smaller left-wing groups on a basis of support for the Russian Bolsheviks. The B.S.P. had been affiliated to the Labour Party since 1916, and it might have seemed natural for the new party also to have secured affiliation as a Socialist society. But the National Executive rejected the application on the ground that the Communist aims were not in accord with the 'constitution, principles, and programme' of the Labour Party.[8] The decision was an indication of the hardening discipline of the party as well as of its hostility to extreme revolutionary tactics. The decision of the Executive was endorsed by a large majority at the 1921 Labour Party Conference.

In 1922 came a new general election and with it the reward for the skilful generalship of Henderson in the preceding eight years. The party increased the number of seats that it contested to 414, which was now over two-thirds of the total. It won altogether 142 of them — almost double its strength at the dissolution, which had already been recruited by successes at by-elections. Although there was a clear Conservative majority in Parliament, in many ways the rise of the Labour Party to a total exceeding that of the broken segments of the Liberal Party was the most important single feature of the election. Furthermore, the new Parliamentary Labour Party contained all the abler leaders of the party, with the very temporary exception of Henderson who had the bad luck again to be defeated (he came in at a by-election in January 1923). Although there were now eighty-five trade-union nominees — which was a considerable increase — it was much more noteworthy that the candidates sponsored by the I.L.P. had won thirty-two seats, as against three in 1918, and that these included not only the anti-war M.P.s such as Mac-Donald and Snowden but also various men of good education such as Clement Attlee and Dr. Alfred Salter. The I.L.P. was also especially successful in Scotland: it won nine seats in Glasgow alone, and the Scottish I.L.P. formed a militant group which was distinctly to the left of the older leaders. In fact, they were the political offspring of the industrial discontent of wartime, which on Clydeside won the support of many of the Irish immigrants. In England, the gains made were less distinctively made by the I.L.P.: the Labour Party did, however, win strength in areas where before the war it had been comparatively weak in the face of Liberalism: notably in Yorkshire and the North-East, and in Greater London. Thus in its success it assumed a more general and national character than before, with M.P.s from all classes of the community — a fitting prelude to its assumption of the rôle of His Majesty's Opposition.

NOTES

1. Hansard, *Parliamentary Debates*, ser. 5, lxv (1831).
2. *Labour Party Annual Report* (1916), pp. 3 f.
3. *Forward*, 10 Feb. 1917, quoted C. T. Solberg, 'The Independent Labour Party, 1893 to 1918' (Oxford B.Litt. thesis), p. 198.
4. Diary, 11 Dec. 1917, M. I. Cole (ed.), *Beatrice Webb's Diaries, 1912–1924* (1952), p. 99.
5. *Labour Party Seventeenth Annual Report* (1918), p. 140.
6. M. I. Cole, *op. cit.* p. 141.
7. George Young, quoted Maddox, *Foreign Relations in British Labour Politics*, p. 74.
8. Henderson to Inkpin, 11 Sept. 1920, quoted in *Labour Party Annual Report* (1921), p. 19.

FURTHER READING

Dr. McKibbin's study, mentioned on p. 34, is the best account of organisational developments. See also Royden Harrison, 'The War Emergency National Workers' Committee, 1914–1920', in A. Briggs and J. Saville, *Essays in Labour History, 1886–1923* (1971); and J. M. Winter, *Socialism and the Challenge of War* (1974). On foreign policy, see W. P. Maddox, for the book already cited; Carl F. Brand, *British Labour's Rise to Power* (Stanford, Calif., 1941); Stephen R. Graubard, *British Labour and the Russian Revolution* (Cambridge, Mass., 1956); and M. Swartz, *The Union of Democratic Control in British Politics during the First World War* (Oxford, 1971). See also Henry Pelling, *America and the British Left* (1956), ch. vii. M. I. Cole (ed.), *Beatrice Webb's Diaries, 1912–1924* (1952) is the most valuable section of the diaries for Labour Party history. Recent research has concentrated on the role of the Fourth Reform Act of 1918. On this, see D. Tanner, *Political Change and the Labour Party, 1900–1918* (Cambridge, 1990) and M. Dawson, 'Money and the real impact of the Fourth Reform Act', *Historical Journal*, xxxv (1992), 369–382. V. L. Allen, 'Reorganisation of the T.U.C., 1918–27', *British Journal of Sociology*, xi (1960), 24–43, is helpful on an allied subject.

CHAPTER IV

The MacDonald Leadership
(1922–31)

(1)

THE years 1922–31 were the years of Ramsay MacDonald's leadership of the Labour Party. The very concept of 'leadership' was something of a novelty: but MacDonald was a leader in a sense that none of his predecessors in the party chairmanship (including himself before the war) had been. From 1922 he was described as not just the 'chairman' of the parliamentary party but as its 'chairman and leader'. The phrase was used to indicate that he was also Leader of the Opposition and potential Prime Minister. The fact that the parliamentary party had established its right to be regarded as the official Opposition in the Commons meant additional prestige and importance for its principal spokesman, who now became the prospective dispenser of government patronage. Similarly, the parliamentary party as a whole considerably increased its standing *vis-à-vis* the trade unions.

MacDonald's elevation by the parliamentary party in place of the incumbent, J. R. Clynes, was a remarkable success, and it could not have happened if the 1922 general election had not completely transformed the character of the parliamentary party. The great change was the increase in the number of Labour M.P.s who were not sponsored by the unions. As we have seen, many of the newcomers were I.L.P. members, and not a few were former Liberals of the U.D.C. type. For them — even for the very militant Clydeside I.L.P.ers — MacDonald had long worn the martyr's crown as the principal opponent of the war. The

Clydeside men were soon to regret their choice, because of the very moderate tone of MacDonald's domestic policies. But by then it was too late: for the 'leader' as he had become benefited from the sturdy loyalty of the trade unionists, who gave him the same trust as they themselves would have expected from the rank and file of a trade union during an industrial strike. The example was set by Henderson and by Clynes himself, who both recognised MacDonald's exceptional parliamentary abilities and served him without rancour.

MacDonald was fully conscious of the character of his task, and of the fact that he was in a completely different position from any earlier chairman of the parliamentary party. Writing to an American friend, he compared his role to that of former Conservative or Liberal Leaders of the Opposition:

> My real difficulty is that with a very small income I have stepped into a job that has never been filled before by anyone who had not a command of much money; and also that whereas my predecessors inherited secretaries and a going machine, I inherited nothing and am having to make everything.[1]

Meanwhile the configuration of the extra-parliamentary party was changing all the time. There were certain formal changes that operated in the direction of increasing the party's discipline and acceptance of leadership from above. The *Herald*, which had been restored as a daily in 1919 and had continued to be a journal of the Left, in 1922 for financial reasons fell under the control of the Labour Party and the T.U.C., and the left-wing George Lansbury ceased to be editor. At the same time the Communist Party with financial help from Moscow emerged as a highly disciplined group on the Left demanding still more insistently to be admitted to affiliation to the Labour Party; and when this was refused, its members attempted to infiltrate and win control of the local Labour Parties. The National Executive found it necessary to respond to this pressure by a

tightening of discipline. By decisions of the party conferences of 1922 to 1925 it ensured that Communists were
debarred from individual membership of the party and from
selection as its parliamentary candidates, although they
could still attend annual conferences as union delegates.
By 1925, however, the Communists and their sympathisers
had already managed to 'capture' quite a number of the
local parties, especially the still rather feeble ones in the
London area; and by the summer of 1927 the National
Executive had had to disaffiliate a total of 23, including 15
in the London area. These rebellious parties were organised by the Communists as a 'National Left Wing Movement'; but this body was outside the Labour Party, and
the expelled local parties were promptly replaced by new
ones formed by the National Executive.

There were, however, certain other changes which went
far to neutralise the increase in formal discipline. One was
the increasing tendency of the major trade-union leaders,
owing to pressure of work, to concentrate their efforts on
the industrial side of the movement and to ignore the
Labour Party. As we have seen, it was now rare for the
secretary of a large trade union to sit in Parliament; and
membership of the General Council was considered to be
incompatible with membership of the National Executive of
the Labour Party. Furthermore, at least one very large
union, the new Transport and General Workers, which had
been created out of the old dockers' unions by Ernest
Bevin, began to regard the House of Commons as nothing
more than a convenient place of retirement for redundant
officials.[2] Such an attitude to parliamentary politics had
an unfavourable effect, not only upon the quality of the
trade-union contribution to the Labour Party, but also
upon the degree of effective co-ordination between the two
sides of the labour movement.

Another centrifugal tendency was apparent in the gradual
evolution of the I.L.P. away from its old position as the
reconciler of unionism and Socialism. The organisation
had not yet suffered any great loss of membership as a

result of the expansion of the role of the local Labour Parties; but it had suffered a change of character. It had become something of a 'cave of Adullam' for Socialists who were impatient with the conservatism of the party's leaders. This characteristic had of course begun to develop on questions of foreign policy during the war years; but with the post-war alternative of individual membership in a local Labour Party, it became apparent that those who deliberately chose to join the I.L.P. were those who wanted a more Socialist and possibly Marxist policy than would be provided by the Henderson-Webb formulae. Even the thorough-going Marxists, unless they were Communists, had to join the I.L.P., now that the old British Socialist Party had disappeared. Leadership for these left-wing Socialists was provided by the Clydesiders, among whom James Maxton was the most prominent; but up till 1924 the old association of MacDonald with the growth of the I.L.P., and the memory of his role during the war, muted any tendency of Maxton and his friends to attack their parliamentary leader, especially so soon after they had played a major part in his selection.

At the end of 1923 Stanley Baldwin, the new Conservative Prime Minister, suddenly dissolved Parliament on the Tariff Reform issue, and a general election ensued. The Labour Party was taken by surprise by these events, but it managed to raise a few more candidates than in 1922, and in an election which swung against the Conservatives (for Tariff Reform was still generally unpopular in Britain) it gained considerably from its position as the larger opposition party in most constituencies. Consequently, although the reunited Liberal Party much improved its position and won 158 seats, the Labour Party also ran further ahead up to a total of 191 seats. The fresh victories were won in areas where the party had remained unusually weak even in 1922: in London alone 15 seats were gained. The I.L.P.-sponsored M.P.s numbered 39, as against 32 in 1922; those sponsored by local Labour Parties increased from 19 to 39. The total of these two — 78 — was beginning to compare with the total trade-union representation, which had moved up merely from 85 to 101.

The Conservatives, with 258 members, were still the largest party in the Commons, but they had no clear majority. As the election had largely been fought on Tariff Reform, which the electorate had rejected, it was clearly the duty of the parties advocating Free Trade to form a government between them, and the Liberals decided to support a Labour Government. In January 1924, therefore, the King called upon MacDonald to form a ministry.

(2)

In choosing his Cabinet, MacDonald at once showed that, while he had plenty of confidence in his own abilities, he did not think very much of his colleagues in the party. He acted as his own Foreign Secretary, and for the offices of Lord President, Lord Chancellor, and First Lord of the Admiralty he went outside the party, bringing in Lord Haldane, the former Liberal minister, Lord Parmoor, a former Conservative M.P., and Lord Chelmsford, also a Conservative. Snowden went to the Exchequer, and Clynes became Lord Privy Seal and Deputy Leader in the Commons. MacDonald tried to keep Henderson out altogether, apparently on the grounds that the ministry would not last long and that Henderson having been defeated (as usual) in the general election could best engage in preparing the party machinery for another contest. But Henderson would not accept this rebuff and insisted on a senior Cabinet post: he obtained the Home Office. The new I.L.P. Left was represented only by John Wheatley, a Clydesider, who became Minister of Health; but the gentle Fred Jowett of Bradford, a left-of-centre I.L.P. member of the older generation, became First Commissioner of Works. On the whole, the trade-union representation was comparatively small — but it was true that there were few suitable trade-union candidates for office.

The new government depended, of course, upon the

Arthur Henderson (1863-1935)

George Lansbury (1859-1940)

support of the Liberals : the possibility of introducing any
sort of Socialist programme was therefore out of the question. But it is doubtful if Snowden, as Chancellor of the
Exchequer, actually wanted to do anything of which the
most orthodox Liberal would have disapproved. His
budget, from the Liberal standpoint, was unimpeachable :
he cut taxes for both rich and poor. Few of the so-called
economic experts of the Labour Party realised the need for
a policy of expansion and public works to deal with the
prevailing unemployment. For the most part, they saw no
remedy short of 'Socialism' which, as they very well knew,
could not be attained in the foreseeable future.

There was, however, one modest success for the Labour
Government in the domestic sphere. This was Wheatley's
Housing Act. This measure, passed of course with Liberal
support, provided for government aid in building council
houses. Under the Act, a good deal of building was initiated, and this had a stimulating effect on the economy,
though most of the effect came only in the later years of
the decade when the Conservatives were again in office.
It was an interesting fact that the one minister to distinguish
himself as a master of the difficult art of securing social
legislation in a minority government, was the one representative of the new I.L.P. Left in the Cabinet.

But by far the greatest success of the government was in
foreign policy. Here, of course, the government could act
more independently of Parliament, and MacDonald soon
justified his decision to be his own Foreign Minister. Faced
by the problem of Franco-German enmity, which had
culminated in the French occupation of the Ruhr, Mac-
Donald now made a friendly approach to Poincaré, the
French Premier. This was a move as shrewd as it was
surprising, for MacDonald might have been expected to
take a very anti-French line on the basis of his known
attitude to the war and to the Versailles Treaty. Poincaré
responded in a friendly fashion, and Anglo-French accord
became even closer when Poincaré's government fell and
Herriot took over. A conference was held in London to

secure the acceptance of the Dawes Plan, whereby an American loan was to underwrite German reparations; and the success of the conference undoubtedly owed much to MacDonald's diplomacy, although it involved an acceptance by the Labour Government of the principle of reparations.

MacDonald's attitude to the League of Nations was at first somewhat ambivalent, for he did not like the fact that the League had originated in the Treaty of Versailles. But he did take the trouble to attend a meeting of the League Assembly at Geneva in September, and he encouraged Henderson and Parmoor to work out a draft treaty for real collective security, in collaboration with representatives of other powers. This draft became known as the Geneva Protocol. Whether a Labour Government would ever have ratified the Protocol, with its commitments to assist in keeping the peace in Europe, is perhaps doubtful: Henderson and Parmoor approved it, of course, but MacDonald seemed lukewarm. The fall of the government, however, left the onus of its rejection to the Conservatives.

There was one further major issue in foreign affairs. This was the question of Anglo-Russian relations. The government made a start by giving unconditional recognition to the Soviet Government; but it proved much more difficult to agree on the terms of financial and commercial agreements. The talks between the Soviet emissaries and the Foreign Office actually broke down and were only resumed as a result of the intervention of a group of Labour M.P.s. This gave the Conservatives an opportunity to argue that the government had given way to left-wing pressure, and a strong anti-Soviet propaganda ensued, which had its effect upon the Liberals.

It was really this issue which brought the government down, although the actual incident which provoked the parliamentary crisis was a trivial matter of domestic politics. J. R. Campbell, the acting editor of a small Communist journal, had published an article urging soldiers not to 'turn your guns on your fellow workers' in industrial disputes. The Attorney-General, Sir Patrick Hastings, decided that this was seditious and a prosecution was initiated. Later on, however, he changed his mind and withdrew the prosecution. The Conservatives, scenting left-wing interference with the judicial process, secured a debate on this issue when the House met in October. Although Hastings effectively answered the charges, MacDonald's defence was unsatisfactory — he had been too absorbed in problems of foreign policy — and a combination of Conservative and Liberal votes defeated the government on a demand for a Select Committee. MacDonald decided to dissolve Parliament and a new general election took place.

The 1924 general election was a notable victory for the Conservatives. Compared with 1923, they won an extra 155 seats. But the Labour Party on balance lost only 40 seats — a little over a fifth of their existing holding. The Liberals bore the brunt, losing 118 and being reduced to a total of 40 — little more than a quarter of the Labour total of 151. It is generally maintained that the Zinoviev letter scare, which took place in election week, significantly affected the polling; but if so, it is difficult to see why the Liberals suffered so heavily rather than the Labour Party. In fact, the Conservatives benefited considerably from their temporary abandonment of Tariff Reform, which won them votes from many who had previously voted Liberal. Consequently, although the Labour vote went up by half a million, it could not keep up with the Conservative success.

On the whole the first Labour Government had performed creditably; and the return of Labour's main opponent in the election was only to be expected after a period of minority rule. But MacDonald had taken too much onto his own shoulders, and he had made one or two errors of tactics, notably in dealing with the Campbell Case and the Zinoviev letter. He had also shown himself very hostile to criticism, particularly from the I.L.P. Both he and his ministers had also signally failed to maintain effective liaison with the T.U.C., and the machinery of the National Joint Council had hardly been used. Consequently, on the morrow of the general election MacDonald's stock, and that of the parliamentary party generally, had considerably sunk within the movement as a whole.

(3)

It was in this situation that the political initiative began to move to the trade-union leaders, who had still not abandoned their hopes of 'direct action'. The General Council had already been showing signs of increased militancy, partly owing to the resignation of some of its more moderate members to join the Labour Government; and in 1925 the Conservative Chancellor of the Exchequer, Winston Churchill, indirectly gave a further impetus to this tendency by putting the country back on the gold standard, which led to a crisis in the coal export trade and demands by the coal-owners for sharp reductions in miners' wages. The miners invoked the aid of the General Council, which in turn promised the support of the transport workers to enforce an embargo on the movement of coal. Faced by this threat, the government gave way in July and agreed to subsidise miners' pay up to 1st May 1926, while a Royal Commission enquired into the problems of the industry. Although the government had made a concession in this instance, it had no intention of doing so again: and it used the intervening months to make preparations in case 1926 should bring a fresh challenge from the T.U.C.

The parliamentary party could do little in the face of the impending industrial conflict. MacDonald knew that if he ventured criticisms of the use of strike action for general political objects, his views would only be indignantly brushed aside by the trade-union militants. The miners were clearly the victims of injustice, and as the other union leaders saw it, their own role was simply a form of sympathetic action to enable the miners to hold their position. The decision to use industrial pressure for political ends was for most of them a decision made unconsciously rather than consciously.

The nine days' General Strike of May 1926 need not be

recounted in detail here. It was, of course, a failure. The
General Council, unlike the government, had made virtually
no preparations for the struggle, and although the withdrawal of labour was almost complete in the industries
concerned, a number of tactical errors were made in issuing
the orders. For instance, it was a mistake to bring out the
printers, as it allowed the government to maintain a mono-
poly of news by means of the wireless. Furthermore, the
General Council had no means of enforcing its demands
in the face of a resolute government, supported as it inevitably was by the great bulk of public opinion. When
it became clear that the government would not yield and
that essential supplies would be kept flowing, there was
nothing that the leaders of the General Council could do ;
and as the days passed they began to realise their dilemma,
and became anxious to find almost any excuse to order a
return to work. The result was that the strike ended in
almost complete defeat, with the miners' dispute — its
original cause — completely unresolved. The miners, who
felt that they had been betrayed, stayed on strike for several
months more, until they finally had to capitulate to the
terms of the mine-owners. But the most important result of
the General Strike for the rest of the labour movement was
the very general recognition that industrial action on so
wide a scale was little short of attempted revolution. The
unions and their leaders in reality had no desire to by-pass
the usual constitutional channels of government, and they
did not try it again. Instead, they began to look once more
upon the parliamentary party as the agent of their political
struggles.

In the immediately following months, the parliamentary
party could not do much more than fight a rearguard action
in defence of the unions. The Conservatives, rather fool-
ishly exploiting their victory, passed a Trade Disputes Act
which retrospectively illegalised the General Strike and imposed the 'contracting-in' system on union members who
wished to pay the political levy to the Labour Party. Owing
to the apathy of union members in general, this considerably

reduced the party's funds until its repeal in 1946.

With the union leadership abandoning its erstwhile militancy, it might have been supposed that the Communist Party would gain supporters among the rank and file; but in fact its success was very limited, although its backing of the miners' cause in the latter months of 1926 won it a few thousand temporary recruits. In 1928 its hard-won gains in the National Left Wing movement and its influence on members of the Labour Party through other propaganda organisations was largely thrown away by a sudden switch of policy adopted on orders of the Communist International in Moscow. The new policy was one of complete sectarianism, involving an abandonment of the 'united front' method of infiltrating the Labour Party, and resulting in a denunciation of both leaders and members of the Labour Party as 'Social Fascists'. Naturally this policy at once reduced Communist influence within the Labour Party to a negligible factor, and entirely prevented the Communist leaders from exploiting the errors and vicissitudes of the Labour Party in the succeeding four years.

The challenge to MacDonald's leadership offered by the I.L.P., however, was of an altogether different order. With a much larger membership and with a long tradition of leadership within the Labour Party — more than two-thirds of the members of the parliamentary party actually held I.L.P. membership — the behaviour of the I.L.P. was of much greater immediate importance. In 1927 the I.L.P. brought forward a new statement of policy, entitled *Socialism in Our Time*. Its principal proposal was for the introduction by a Labour Government of a 'Living Wage' — a minimum wage which would help to stimulate consumption and so revitalise the national economy. In shaping this programme the I.L.P. had had the advice of J. A. Hobson, one of the ablest economists of the time and in many ways a Keynesian before Keynes. There was nothing particularly extreme about this: but now that the I.L.P. was led by Maxton and others who were equally given to uncompromising utterances, there was little chance of the new programme being accepted by the Labour Party as a whole. At the 1927 Labour Party Conference it was opposed not only by MacDonald and Snowden, with their rigidly orthodox economic ideas, but also by many of the trade-union leaders, who felt that it might in some way or other adversely affect their sectional interests.

It was at the 1927 conference that the I.L.P. made clear its disapproval of MacDonald, by refusing to nominate him for the post of Treasurer of the Labour Party which he had held since 1912. The following year the Labour Party conference adopted a rather vague policy statement called *Labour and the Nation*, which was in no way an advance and in some ways a retreat from the earlier statement, *Labour and the New Social Order*, prepared by Henderson and Webb in 1918. Thereafter, the rift between I.L.P. policy and Labour Party policy seemed unbridgeable, and a struggle ensued on the question of whether I.L.P.-sponsored M.P.s should support the policy of the I.L.P. or that of the Labour Party.

This conflict was unresolved when in 1929 the term of the Conservative Government drew towards its close and a new general election took place. The Labour Party benefited from the popular feeling of dissatisfaction with the existing economic situation, and especially the chronic unemployment. The party's M.P.s in the new House totalled 288, which made it for the first time the largest party, although still with no clear majority. Among the 288 there was an enormous increase in the total sponsored by divisional Labour Parties — 128 as against 25 in 1924. This was partly due to the weakness of the unions after the passing of the Trade Disputes Act, and partly to the secession from the I.L.P. of candidates who could not agree with its sectional attitude. But in addition, any general electoral swing towards Labour was likely to result in specially marked gains for the local Labour Parties, because their candidates, unlike those of the unions, tended to be concentrated in the marginal or unfavourable constituencies. For the first time, trade-union-sponsored M.P.s numbered less than half the total, being only 115 out of 288. I.L.P.-sponsored successes numbered 36, almost half of them being in Scotland, and the Co-operative Party won 9 seats. As for the geographical distribution of the party in general, considerable progress was again made in the London area, and the depression in the Lancashire cotton trade enabled it to win 39 seats there, as against 18 in 1924. The verdict of the electorate clearly was that the Labour Party should be allowed another attempt at government.

(4)

MacDonald's Cabinet included most of those who had served in 1924, although Haldane, on whom MacDonald had previously relied for details of procedure, had died in 1928. The new Cabinet was constructed in consultation with Thomas, the Railwaymen's leader, Snowden, and Henderson. Henderson insisted on the Foreign Office, and MacDonald conceded it somewhat reluctantly, having toyed with the idea of appointing the rather more pliant Thomas to the post. Snowden returned to the Exchequer and Thomas became Lord Privy Seal. Wheatley and Jowett, who were identified with the policy of the I.L.P., were both dropped, but Lansbury was taken in instead as a representative of the Left. An important novelty was that Thomas, assisted by a three-man committee, was appointed to draw up plans to deal with unemployment. The three assistants were Lansbury (whose department was the Office of Works), Thomas Johnston (Under-Secretary for Scotland), and Oswald Mosley (Chancellor of the Duchy of Lancaster).

MacDonald realised his own and his colleagues' weakness on economic affairs and in 1930 established an Economic Advisory Council, consisting of economists, industrialists, and others to advise him on economic problems. Unfortunately, the experts could not agree and Snowden preferred to follow the recommendations of his Treasury officials. Meanwhile, the unemployment figures continued to rise, and by the autumn of 1930 exceeded two million.

The only minister to demand action, even at the expense of his office, was Mosley, who proposed state control of foreign trade and the expansion of purchasing power in the home market. When this was not accepted, he resigned from the government, being replaced by Clement Attlee.

As in 1924, MacDonald's main interest was in diplomacy. Although Henderson was Foreign Secretary, the Prime Minister reserved for himself the control of naval disarmament negotiations and other matters which principally involved Anglo-American relations. The Washington Naval Treaty of 1922 was expiring, but there was difficulty in reaching a fresh agreement. On taking office, MacDonald at once cut the British naval building programme and then personally visited America to discuss the terms of a new treaty. This led to a five-power conference in London in January 1930, which resulted in agreed reductions in their forces by Britain, America, and Japan, though not by France and Italy. MacDonald also showed keen interest in the development of self-government in India, and took the responsibility for the Viceroy's declaration that 'Dominion status' was the goal of British policy there. After the report of the Simon Commission in 1930, a Round Table Conference on the future of India was summoned for the autumn of 1930, but it had to be adjourned early in 1931, largely owing to the refusal of the Indian National Congress to take part. MacDonald persevered, however, and arranged for a resumption in the autumn in the expectation that Congress delegates would then attend.

In other matters of foreign policy, Henderson was in charge. One of the distinctive things he did, at the instigation of his Under-Secretary, Hugh Dalton, was to distribute copies of *Labour and the Nation* to permanent officials in the Foreign Office. His main achievements were: a commercial treaty with Russia, following a resumption of diplomatic relations; the withdrawal of occupation forces from the Rhineland and a resumption of work on preparations for a general disarmament conference; the signature of the optional clause of the Statute for the Permanent

Court of International Justice, accepting compulsory arbitration in international disputes; and a complete change in policy towards Egypt, though falling short of an Anglo-Egyptian Treaty owing to difficulties about the status of the Sudan. Henderson's work laid the groundwork for effective international agreements on various outstanding issues, but it was his misfortune — and everyone else's — that the onset of the economic depression upset the will of the nations to reach agreement.

Meanwhile the government's domestic policies were proving singularly unsuccessful. The legislative programme was crippled either by Liberal opposition in the Commons or by Conservative opposition in the Lords. This would not have damaged the Labour Party if the government had produced a reasonable plan for grappling with the great issue of unemployment, and had either secured its approval by Parliament or resigned. But in fact, nothing effective was even agreed by the Cabinet. Naturally, this exacerbated dissension within the party. The annual conference of 1930 saw a powerful challenge from Mosley, whose Memorandum had been rejected by the Cabinet; and a resolution supporting his policy was only narrowly defeated. Within the parliamentary party there was also trouble, some of it with Mosley and some of it with the I.L.P. Mosley actually founded a New Party, to which he won over four other Labour M.P.s, and this resulted in their expulsion. At the same time, the I.L.P. was seeking to force its M.P.s to obey its own policy decisions rather than those of the Labour Party; and negotiations on this vexed question between the Labour Party National Executive and the leaders of the I.L.P. took place in 1930 and were still dragging on when the government fell in 1931.

The international financial crisis which brought the government down occurred in the summer of 1931. The collapse in May of the Credit Anstalt, a bank in Vienna, led to a loss of confidence and a drain of gold from London, where many foreign banks held short-term investments. In August the government faced the alternatives of abandon-

66

ing the gold standard or securing fresh loans in Paris and
New York; but the New York bankers would only help if
they were sure that the government was taking sufficient
measures of retrenchment to restore confidence on orthodox
lines. This meant, in fact, cuts in civil service pay and in
the pay of the forces, and also in employment benefits. A
substantial minority of the Cabinet would not accept the
unemployment cuts; but the only alternative seemed to be
a revenue tariff, and this was impracticable as the Liberals
would not have accepted it.

Under the circumstances of the crisis, with a serious
division in the Cabinet, it was decided to consult the
National Executive of the party and also the General
Council of the T.U.C. This was done on 20th August,
when both bodies were summoned to hear statements by
MacDonald and Snowden. After a few questions the meeting broke up, so that the two bodies could consider their
attitude separately; and the General Council sent a small
delegation, including Citrine, the T.U.C. secretary, and
Bevin, the secretary of the big new amalgamation, the
Transport and General Workers Union, to tell Snowden
that they could not agree to the cuts. As Sidney Webb
told his wife: 'The General Council are pigs. They won't
agree to any cuts.'[3] MacDonald began to talk about the
possibility of a Coalition Government, although the members of his Cabinet demurred.

On 23rd August MacDonald resigned office, and early
next morning he accepted the King's commission to form
a new government with the support of the Liberals and
Conservatives. He announced his decision to his aston-
ished Labour colleagues later the same morning. No discussion took place; the ministers who were not joining the
new Cabinet trooped off together, and later that day a
'Council of War', as Dalton calls it in his memoirs, met
in the party secretary's room at Transport House (the new
party and T.U.C. headquarters) to rally the party in
opposition to MacDonald's new government. Those present besides Henderson, the party secretary, were Lansbury,

who had also been in the Cabinet, Citrine and Bevin, Middleton, the assistant secretary of the party, and Francis Hirst, who was chairman of the National Executive and also, incidentally, a member of Bevin's union. 'This is like the General Strike,' said Bevin, 'I'm prepared to put everything in'; and then the group sent for a representative of the *Daily Herald,* whose policy was under the joint control of the party and the T.U.C., in order to 'settle the line of tomorrow's leader'.[4] A new era in the history of the party had begun : the MacDonald era was over; the control of the party was passing to the extra-parliamentary organs again, and to the T.U.C.

(5)

For nine years MacDonald had dominated the Labour Party, and for nine years he had held an authority which no single individual had ever possessed over its members before. He had received great loyalty from the parliamentary party, and not least from the trade unionists. But the final demands of the 1931 crisis were too great a strain on that loyalty.

The rights and wrongs of the conflict between MacDonald and his party have been debated bitterly ever since. Was MacDonald a 'traitor' to his party or was he the 'saviour' of his country ? We can probably allow him at least an honesty of purpose. He knew very little about economics and had to rely upon Snowden, who was a broken reed. He had devoted the previous two years to external affairs and diplomacy and had simply not kept in touch, either with domestic affairs generally or with the rank and file of the labour movement. Consequently, he exaggerated the gravity of the financial crisis and overestimated his own influence inside the labour movement. He expected to carry about half the parliamentary party with him into his so-called 'National' government; but when his supporters were all counted, they amounted to only Snowden and Thomas, his colleagues in the new government, his son Malcolm, and four others.

The MacDonald Leadership (1922–31)

It has been said that in this crisis the trade-union leaders acted with narrow selfishness, determined to refuse any sort of sacrifice by their members even though the country was in the direst straits. Of course, the trade-union leaders did have sectional interests to serve, but it is noteworthy that the ablest of them — in particular, Bevin and Citrine — understood a great deal more about economics than Mac-Donald and Snowden did, and had an idea of how absurd the whole crisis was. Bevin had been a member of Mac-Donald's Economic Advisory Council and had really paid attention to the discussions, and especially to what was being said by Keynes and G. D. H. Cole. When he disagreed with MacDonald, he knew what he was talking about. But the abstract problems of economic theory were not widely understood at the time. The firmness of the trade-union leadership, and the lack of contact between MacDonald and his parliamentary following, saw to it that when the immediate crisis was over MacDonald was left on one side, in the office of Prime Minister, but virtually without personal supporters ; and on the other side was all but a tiny fragment of the Labour Party and the whole trade-union movement, united in bitter opposition, and under a new and very different leadership.

NOTES

1. MacDonald to O. G. Villard, 15 Jan. 1923, quoted by M. S. Venkataramani in *Political Studies*, viii (1961), 237.

2. Alan Bullock, *Life and Times of Ernest Bevin*, i (1960), 204.

3. Diary, 22 Aug. 1931, M. I. Cole (ed.), *Beatrice Webb's Diaries, 1924–1932* (1956), p. 281.

4. Hugh Dalton, *Call Back Yesterday* (1953), p. 274.

FURTHER READING

R. W. Lyman has provided a most judicious study of the 1924 government in his *First Labour Government, 1924* (1957). This may be read in conjunction with a later-published memorandum on the subject by Sidney Webb, for which see *Political Quarterly*, xxxii (1961). R. Skidelsky, *Politicians and the Slump* (1967) is a valuable study of the Second Labour Government; but its 'neo-Keynesianism' is ably criticised in R. McKibbin, 'The Economic Policy of the Second Labour Government 1929–1931', *Past and Present*, 68 (1975). David Marquand's official biography, *Ramsay MacDonald* (1977), is naturally of importance throughout. There is still useful material in the strongly pro-MacDonald study by R. Bassett, *1931: Political Crisis* (1958). D. Carlton, *MacDonald versus Henderson* (1970) examines the foreign policy of the Second Labour Government from original sources. The following works are useful for the light they throw on events within the labour movement at this time : Fenner Brockway, *Inside the Left* (1942) ; Lord Citrine, *Men and Work* (1964) ; M. I. Cole (ed.), *Beatrice Webb's Diaries, 1924–1932* (1956) ; Arthur Marwick, *Clifford Allen* (1964). Arthur Marwick has also written a succinct analysis of 'The Independent Labour Party in the Nineteen-Twenties', *Bulletin of the Institute of Historical Research*, xxxv (1962). See also R. E. Dowse, 'The Left Wing Opposition During the First Two Labour Governments', *Parliamentary Affairs*, xiv (1960–1) and 'The I.L.P. and Foreign Politics, 1918–23', *International Review of Social History*, vii (1962). For the Communist Party, see Henry Pelling, *British Communist Party: A Historical Profile* (1958). Two useful books on the General Strike, in addition to the works by Bullock and Citrine, are Julian Symons, *The General Strike* (1957) and Christopher Farman, *The General Strike* (1972).

CHAPTER V

Convalescence : The General Council's Party
(1931-40)

(1)

ON 25th August 1931 the T.U.C. and the extra-parliamentary party took control of the parliamentary party and disavowed the leadership of MacDonald. The main political crisis was over, so far as the Labour Party was concerned : but its consequences still had to be worked out. The parliamentary party's Consultative Committee, which had been its liaison committee with the Labour Cabinet, held two meetings with the National Executive and the General Council of the T.U.C. before, on 28th August, a full meeting of the parliamentary party took place. And when the parliamentary party did meet, it met at Transport House, with the members of the General Council of the T.U.C. present. According to Dalton, this was 'an innovation, suggested by Uncle [Henderson] to mark unity'.[1] One may suspect, however, that it was an innovation designed to *preserve* unity — by intimidating the waverers. Only one of the four Labour members of MacDonald's new Cabinet attended : this was Lord Sankey, who was heard out respectfully but who won no support. Henderson was elected leader of the parliamentary party by an overwhelming majority.

The influence of the General Council and particularly of Bevin, its dominating personality, on the fortunes of the Labour Party at this juncture has perhaps not been properly appreciated. Bevin had established his claim to rank as a national leader by his effective role in the General Strike. Now aged 50, he was at the height of his powers, and his position inside his own union, the Transport and General Workers, was supreme, for he had by now consolidated the amalgamations of the early 1920's which were also his own work. He had been responsible for building Transport House, which from the date of its completion in 1928 was for a generation not only the headquarters of his union, but also the home of both the T.U.C. and the Labour Party. In 1929, as chairman of the board of the *Daily Herald*, he had made the agreement with Odhams whereby the paper obtained fresh capital and rose to a circulation of well over a million. In theory, the politics of the paper were controlled by the T.U.C. and the Labour Party, but in practice this meant Bevin, as was generally acknowledged. It is true that he was not an M.P.; but his union had sponsored twelve of the existing members of the parliamentary party. He was not on the National Executive; but a member of his union, Hirst, was at the time its chairman, and as such was to be chairman of the forthcoming annual conference of the party. Finally, at the party conference, the Transport and General Workers would have a vote of 235,000, which was almost 10 per cent of the total vote of all the delegates present.

It is true, of course, that Henderson still had great influence. He was still secretary of the party, as he had been for twenty years, and he had been the leader of the Cabinet minority opposed to MacDonald. But Henderson's role in the crisis was not as decisive as Bevin's. As always, Henderson was opposed to a complete break with Mac-Donald. He had not fully made up his mind to leave the Cabinet on the question of unemployment cuts until he had heard the views of Bevin and Citrine; and he still hoped that there would be no final separation of MacDonald from the party, but rather a temporary divergence like what had happened during the war. Finally, Henderson had only become leader of the parliamentary party with considerable reluctance. He was now 68 and he did not feel that he was ever likely to take office again.

Meanwhile, MacDonald, almost devoid of supporters

from the Parliamentary Labour Party, found himself a prisoner of his new allies. In September the new government went off the gold standard without greatly upsetting the City, although the Labour Cabinet had been warned that such an act was quite unthinkable. Later that month the Conservatives began to increase their pressure for a general election. Neville Chamberlain, who was the most vigorous of the Conservative leaders, sought to retain MacDonald while getting rid of the Liberals: this would enable them to win the election and then go for Tariff Reform. But MacDonald did not like the idea. As Sir Clive Wigram, the King's Private Secretary, wrote to the King on 28th September:

> He does not like the idea of smashing up the Labour Party at the head of a Conservative association. He does not know how to run with the hares and hunt with the hounds. He has hopes of sitting tight now and attracting a following of the Labour Party. This may take a long time.[2]

On the same day, however, the National Executive met and formally expelled MacDonald and his colleagues from the Labour Party. It did not look as if there was much prospect of 'attracting a following of the Labour Party'.

Under these circumstances, MacDonald began to think of perpetuating the Coalition by fighting a general election and perhaps thereby building up his little National Labour group. He could not contemplate this without Liberal support; but the Conservatives, who were anxious to introduce Tariff Reform, did not really want to keep the Liberals in the Coalition. Eventually, a compromise was reached; the Liberals stayed in, but agreed to an election in which they would put forward their own slightly different programme. But so far as possible, the fiscal issue would be avoided in the campaign; all National candidates would seek a general mandate, a 'doctor's mandate' as it was called, to deal with the financial crisis. On these terms, a dissolution took place and the general election followed before the end of October.

The election was marked by a bitter campaign against the Labour Party, conducted by all the National candidates but in particular by the Labour Party's own former leaders. Snowden made a truly remarkable election broadcast, in which he spoke of the Labour Party's policy — very little different from what he himself had advocated for years — as 'Bolshevism run mad'. In the majority of contests there was only one National candidate, who obtained the united vote of the Conservative and Liberal parties, together with any Labour vote which had followed MacDonald and Snowden. Thus even if the Labour poll had been as large as in 1929 the party would have lost many of its seats. In fact, the Labour poll dropped from 8 million to 6 million — not such a large fall, considering all that had happened — but its parliamentary position was staggeringly weakened. Only forty-six official party members returned to the new Commons, together with five I.L.P. representatives who had fought the election separately. MacDonald and his little National Labour group numbered thirteen in the new House, but both Mosley's New Party and the Communists failed to win a single seat.

Of the old Labour Government, Lansbury was the only Cabinet minister to survive on the opposition side; and there were only two junior ministers left, Attlee and Sir Stafford Cripps, who had been Solicitor-General. As is usual when the parliamentary party is at the bottom of its fortunes, most of its members were trade unionists, especially miners. In fact, exactly half the party consisted of candidates sponsored by the Miners Federation. The only area of the country which now had any large proportion of Labour M.P.s was South Wales, where about a third of the party had their seats. It was no wonder that the parliamentary party failed to retain the prestige and authority that it had held inside the labour movement in the preceding decade.

(2)

For the first year of the new Parliament Henderson continued as titular leader, but as he was not in the Commons and was in any case spending much time in Geneva as President of the Disarmament Conference, Lansbury served as acting leader with Attlee as his deputy. In the autumn of 1932 Henderson resigned the leadership, though he remained secretary of the extra-parliamentary party; and Lansbury now became titular as well as actual leader in the House. But obviously the parliamentary party was a poor and nerveless thing in this Parliament of the early 1930's. Lansbury himself was already 72, and was in any case a poor leader because of his tendency towards a woolly-minded sentimentality. His two ablest assistants, Attlee and Cripps, both seemed to be suffering from the shock of the electoral defeat, and inclined to advocate policies of extreme and barren militancy. Cripps, for instance, made speeches about the 'sinister influence' of Buckingham Palace and the need for a temporary dictatorship by the party if Labour should win a general election. Attlee was more discreet in his utterances, but his views were almost as extreme. These two men were both public school men (Attlee had been at Haileybury, Cripps at Winchester) and it took time for them to establish relations of trust, either with their other parliamentary colleagues on the one hand, or with the extra-parliamentary movement on the other. At first Lansbury was the only member of the parliamentary party to sit on the National Executive, which he did by virtue of his position as parliamentary leader; and the liaison with the bulk of the trade-union world — except the Miners Federation — was also poor.

Under these conditions, it might be supposed that the I.L.P. would find its way back into the Labour Party. What the I.L.P. leaders had originally objected to, after all, was the conservatism of the Labour Party's programme and policy in the days of MacDonald. But this had turned into an assertion of the I.L.P.'s right to determine its M.P.s' voting behaviour as a separate group in the House of Commons. When this was denied, its candidates fought the 1931 election as a separate group, and in 1932 by conference decision the I.L.P. disaffiliated from the Labour Party. Thus was ended an association which had been continuous from the foundation of the Labour Party, and which had indeed been largely responsible for the Labour Party's successful establishment. But things had changed radically in the 1920's. The I.L.P. had become an extremist group, largely centred upon Clydeside; and the effect of disaffiliation, while damaging to the Labour Party, was catastrophic to the I.L.P. Many of its older members at once resigned, and others soon came to realise that it had no future as an electoral rival to the Labour Party. From almost 17,000 members in 1932 the total steadily declined to a mere 4400 in 1935.

With the loss of the I.L.P., it was natural that attempts should be made to found a new Socialist society within the Labour Party, for those who wished to devise and propagate an advanced Socialist programme. Two small groups had already come into existence: one of them was the New Fabian Research Bureau, which was intended to revitalise the long moribund Fabian Society; the other was the Society for Socialist Inquiry and Propaganda, which was really for the dissemination of the research undertaken by the other body. The N.F.R.B. continued its work and finally in 1939 was reunited with the Fabian Society, giving the older body new energy and receiving in return the remaining assets of the Society. But the S.S.I.P. was amalgamated with a group which left the I.L.P. when it disaffiliated from the Labour Party, and was reconstituted as the Socialist League, with E. F. Wise, from the I.L.P., as its first chairman. Wise died suddenly in 1933, and soon it was being run by Stafford Cripps. Unlike the N.F.R.B., it soon began to run into conflict with the policy of the party and looked as if it would repeat the later history of the I.L.P.

In this period of disorder among the more committed

Socialists and intellectuals, the General Council of the
T.U.C. under the leadership of Bevin and Citrine abandoned
its usual role of being the sheet-anchor of the party and
instead moved in to take the helm. Citrine demanded that
'the General Council should be regarded as having an
integral right to initiate and participate in any political
matter which it deems to be of direct concern to its constituents'.[3] For this purpose the National Joint Council,
which had originally been established in 1921, was reconstituted on a new basis. Instead of the General Council,
the parliamentary party, and the National Executive having
equal representation on it, it was remodelled so that the
General Council alone appointed half of the members.
Henceforward it was to meet at least once a month, and
also was to be summoned in any emergency requiring
prompt action. Although its purpose was theoretically only
consultative, in fact its decisions were bound to carry great
authority inside the movement, and it would have been
highly embarrassing for the parliamentary party or any
other body inside the party to have gone counter to it on
any major issue.

The records show that the National Council of Labour
was constantly meeting in the 1930's and constantly issuing
statements on policy, and Bevin himself, who served on it
from 1931 to 1937, regarded these decisions as binding even
upon the parliamentary leader. In 1933, for instance, he
wrote to Lansbury to protest against his speaking on the
platform of the Socialist League without getting prior permission from the National Council of Labour. On this
occasion Lansbury dug in his rather weary toes. 'I do not
think', he replied, 'that I am called upon to ask permission
from anybody to do this — and certainly have no intention
of doing so.'[4] At the same time, he made no attempt to
assert his own authority as parliamentary leader. At the
1934 party conference, he even admitted that he did not
regard himself as the 'leader', but rather as no more than
the 'spokesman', of the party.[5]

With the expansion of Japan in the Far East and the

rise to power of Hitler in Germany in 1933, foreign policy began to assume a new urgency, and it was in this sphere that the most serious divergencies began to appear between the parliamentary 'spokesman' and the National Council of Labour. Lansbury was a pacifist with Marxian undertones: he was not only opposed to the use of armaments for self-defence, but to the very existence of the League of Nations, which he regarded as a society of rich powers banded against the 'have-nots'. The union leaders, on the other hand, took a more practical view of foreign affairs based upon their industrial experience, and regarded collective security through the League as the equivalent of collective bargaining through a trade union. Although Henderson had great hopes of disarmament, this was also in reality his view. But he was now too old and infirm to be of much assistance. He had been re-elected to Parliament in 1933, but in 1934 he resigned the secretaryship of the party and in 1935 he died.

Henderson's resignation from the secretaryship opened up the whole question of the future control of the political side of the movement; for although in the previous three years he had largely ceased to exercise control as he had done in the past, particularly during and just after the war, it was clear that a younger man might reassert power in this office. After the party's misfortunes with MacDonald, however, there was a strong tendency to mistrust any concentration of power in the hands of one man. It was therefore decided that Henderson's successor should not be allowed to become a Member of Parliament. This ruled out Herbert Morrison, probably the most powerful contender, who had built up the London Labour Party to such a degree of strength that in this same year it was able to win control of the London County Council — a control which it never lost. But it also ruled out other possible contenders with parliamentary ambitions. In the upshot, the choice fell upon Jimmy Middleton, the quiet-spoken official who had been assistant secretary ever since 1903. After this, it was many years before the post of secretary again assumed major importance: but the National Executive to some extent gained in collective weight.

After this, then, there was a rough division of policy-making functions between the National Council of Labour (dominated by Bevin and Citrine) and the National Executive (dominated by politicians, but elected by the union block vote at annual conferences). The National Council determined the outlines of policy, declaring for collective security, opposition to Fascism, refusal to collaborate with the Communists in a new 'United Front', and so on. The National Executive had a powerful Policy Sub-Committee, consisting of Attlee and Cripps, who were now on the National Executive, and the other leading younger contenders for parliamentary honours, several of them still being outside Parliament: Herbert Morrison, Hugh Dalton, Arthur Greenwood. The Sub-Committee was very active in drawing up detailed legislative and administrative programmes for a Labour Government, within the general policies laid down by the Council of Labour. The concept of 'planning' was only now being evolved, and the Labour Party's economic experts were just awakening to the need to prepare every step of their proposed transition to Socialism, in such a way that the economy would continue to function satisfactorily throughout. In this process of reshaping policy, the Roosevelt New Deal, the Russian Five-Year Plan, and even the work of Schacht in Nazi Germany, all had their impact.

In 1935 it seemed that a new general election was imminent; and while the results of the election would, it was hoped, provide an opportunity for the improvement of the parliamentary leadership, it was the parliamentary leadership which had to conduct the election campaign. The dilemma was a real one, for the party could not rely upon Lansbury to provide a skilful management of the election, or even to follow party policy in his own utterances. It has already been pointed out that his attitude on foreign policy was in conflict with that of the party; and with Mussolini's impending attack upon Abyssinia, foreign affairs had assumed the highest importance. The 'Peace Ballot', conducted in the course of the summer by members of the League of Nations Union, showed that there was in fact a remarkably strong sentiment in the country in favour of 'sanctions' by the League, if necessary involving the use of force. To continue to have a pacifist as leader of the party would only lead to misunderstandings: yet Lansbury resisted all hints that it was time for him to resign. The issue came to a head at the 1935 annual conference of the party, when Lansbury opposed a resolution reaffirming the policy laid down by the National Council of Labour. Ernest Bevin, speaking immediately after Lansbury, accused him directly of 'hawking your conscience around from body to body asking to be told what you ought to do with it'. The resolution was carried by an overwhelming majority, and Lansbury thereupon resigned. He was replaced by Attlee on a temporary basis for the remainder of the parliamentary session; and so Attlee acted as leader during the general election which took place in November. For the first time the Labour Party's chief spokesman was not a man of working-class origin.

The election was fought by the National Government very largely on the issue of foreign policy, and on the question of collective security Baldwin, who was now Prime Minister in place of MacDonald, very largely stole the Labour Party's thunder. The result was that although the Labour Party made a considerable recovery, it still did not get back even to its 1929 strength. Its total poll was over 8 million again, but the Conservatives alone got almost 10½ million. The Labour Party did well once more in the London area and recovered much lost ground in Yorkshire and Scotland. The total number of seats won was 154, of which 79 were won by trade-union-sponsored candidates: a majority but only a small majority this time. Many of the abler members of the 1929 Parliament now reappeared — Morrison, Dalton, and Emanuel Shinwell included. The National Labour group led by MacDonald sank to eight, MacDonald himself being defeated by Shinwell; and one

Communist, Willie Gallacher, was elected. The I.L.P. retained four seats, all in Glasgow, but was obviously a waning force. It could safely be asserted that the electorate showed little sympathy for splinter groups on the Left or for that matter on the Right.

(3)

The first issue to face the new parliamentary party was that of its own leadership. Clynes had been re-elected to the Commons, but he was now 66 and so could hardly expect a long term in the office. He refused to stand. This left three main contenders — Attlee, the incumbent, described by the *New Statesman* as 'a natural Adjutant, but not a General'; Arthur Greenwood, a former economics lecturer who had been Minister of Health in the 1929 government; and Herbert Morrison, once a Cockney errand-boy but also a former minister. Morrison was supported by Dalton and also had the backing of many London members; Greenwood was supported by Bevin, who had clashed with Morrison, and probably by the newly-elected trade unionists generally; Attlee was backed by the re-elected M.P.s who had grown to like him in the previous Parliament. On a first vote, Attlee got 58 votes, Morrison 44, and Greenwood 33; on a second vote Attlee secured almost all Greenwood's votes, partly because he was still thought to be only a temporary leader. But he grew in authority and gradually consolidated his position, profiting by the rivalries of the other potential candidates, and gradually winning the respect of Bevin and other union leaders outside the House.

For a time, however, there was still a distinct contrast between the National Council of Labour's policy of collective security and the actual attitude of the parliamentary party, which continued to oppose the defence estimates. The parliamentary party always contained a number of out-and-out pacifists, and anti-militarist feeling remained strong in its ranks: this had an effect on the party's decisions as to particular issues in the House. But in 1936

Dalton, who was keen on rearmament, was chairman of the National Executive, and Bevin was simultaneously chairman of the General Council. Between them they contrived to swing the policy of the parliamentary party, being assisted in this by the outbreak of the Spanish Civil War. Their method of action was as follows: a strong statement was made by the National Council of Labour in the summer; this was then endorsed by the Trades Union Congress which as usual met early in September. The Labour Party Conference followed a month later in October — a practice initiated in 1924 when it had been postponed from June owing to the difficulty of Members of Parliament attending before the House had risen. It was difficult, therefore, for Conference not to follow the strong lead given by the National Council of Labour and by Congress — as Herbert Morrison found on this particular occasion, which committed the movement to the support of the existing rearmament programme. Morrison was resisting throughout the summer but when the conference met in October he did not speak, and the resolution was easily carried.

The Spanish Civil War aroused public opinion within the labour movement to a degree that no foreign war had ever done before, unless we go back to the American Civil War. There was widespread enthusiasm for the Spanish Republicans, as against the army clique led by General Franco, and although at first the National Council of Labour advocated non-intervention, this policy was soon abandoned as it was seen to be ineffective. The Communist Party, now rapidly growing in strength since the abandonment of its sectarian policy in 1933, acted as recruiting agent for the International Brigade, which had been established on the orders of the Communist International. Many young men, not only Communist Party members or sympathisers, went off to join the Brigade or to work behind the lines, and a considerable impetus was given to the policy of the 'United Front' of all parties on the Left against the threat of Fascism. The mood of the times was exemplified by the sensational success of the Left Book Club, founded by Victor Gollancz to advocate this cause.

The growth of Socialist sympathies in all sections of the population since 1931 had by no means failed to benefit the Labour Party itself. The individual membership of the party had doubled in the years 1928 to 1937, and the only trouble was that the Socialist League, which had replaced the I.L.P. as an affiliated Socialist society, was showing much the same hostility to general conference decisions as its predecessor had done. The Socialist League wished to form a 'United Front' with the Communists and the I.L.P., but this was resisted by the National Council of Labour, as the union officials and the more senior Labour Party leaders had a vivid recollection of the trouble that they had had from the Communists in earlier years. Besides, as they realised, the Communists would have been a heavy liability for the Labour Party at election time.

A Constituency Parties Movement, led by a rank-and-file activist called Ben Greene, developed to demand separately-elected representation on the National Executive. Hugh Dalton, who was Chairman of the Executive in 1936–7, decided that this was a desirable change to make, as it would weaken bodies like the I.L.P. and the Socialist League. It also meant a slight reduction in the power of the unions, but Dalton persuaded Bevin to agree and it was introduced at the 1937 conference. The number of seats made available to the constituency parties was simultaneously increased from five to seven. It was also decided to move the conference date to Whitsuntide to avoid immediately following the T.U.C. The new Executive election system came into force at once, and one or two representatives of the intellectual Left at once appeared on the National Executive, in particular Harold Laski and D. N. Pritt. But only one or two : as Dalton had foreseen, these representatives were largely the prisoners of the National Executive majority ; and the conference then proceeded to disaffiliate the Socialist League and to reject the policy of the 'United Front'. Cripps

83

knew that he had been beaten and he decided upon a voluntary dissolution of the Socialist League.

The final effort of Cripps and others to collaborate with the Communists and the I.L.P. came in 1939. By this time the effort was somewhat quixotic, for the Communist Party had been not a little discredited by the behaviour of the Communists in Spain in attacking their Anarchist comrades-in-arms, and also by Stalin's purges of the Russian army and Comintern hierarchy. Nevertheless, Cripps, who was himself a wealthy man as a result of his success at the bar, decided to conduct a nation-wide campaign for what was now called the 'Popular Front'. This led to his expulsion from the Labour Party by the National Executive, with only two dissentients (Ellen Wilkinson and Pritt, but not Laski). His principal followers, Charles Trevelyan, Aneurin Bevan, and George Strauss, were also expelled. This action was endorsed by an overwhelming majority by the party conference.

By this time the danger of war had become acute. At the time of Munich the National Council of Labour had spoken out against concessions to Hitler; and Churchill is said to have telephoned Attlee on 20th September 1938 to tell him 'Your declaration does honour to the British nation'.[6] On several occasions, deputations of the three executives of the Labour movement — the parliamentary party, the National Executive and the General Council — called upon Chamberlain or Halifax, his Foreign Minister, to discuss the situation and to demand a change of policy. This only came in March, when the occupation of Prague by the Germans finally convinced the government that Hitler was quite untrustworthy.

Almost immediately afterwards, the government decided to introduce conscription. Although the Labour Party had accepted the need for rearmament since 1937 — which was not too bad a record for an opposition party interested in social reform and provided with very little information on defence questions by the government — it seemed to show considerable weakness in maintaining its hostility to conscription. Continuing suspicion of Chamberlain's intentions had a good deal to do with this. As soon as the measure was passed, the labour movement accepted it quite loyally; and Attlee has subsequently admitted that he thinks the attempt to prevent it was a mistake.[7] At the time, Dalton and a few others refused to vote against it in the House — exercising the conscience clause for a very different purpose from that for which it had been introduced.

(4)

On 1st September Hitler invaded Poland and two days later Britain declared war. In the mounting crisis immediately preceding the declaration, the National Council of Labour had been meeting, and a committee consisting of Dalton, Morrison, and Citrine had been appointed to confer with the Prime Minister (Attlee being ill at the time). On 2nd September a joint meeting of the National Executive and of the Executive of the parliamentary party decided that the party should not join the government. The General Council of the T.U.C. had no part in this decision because the T.U.C. was just then taking place at Bridlington. But there was no possibility of disagreement on the issue. Shortly afterwards, an electoral truce was agreed upon as in 1914.

Although Chamberlain secured the co-operation of Churchill and other Conservative dissentients in reconstructing his government, the hostility between the National Government and the Labour Opposition remained strong. Moreover, there seemed to be plenty to criticise in the conduct of the war. A distinct air of complacency was noticeable in Whitehall during what became known as 'the phoney war'. It was only in April 1940, just after Chamberlain had made a speech saying that Hitler 'had missed the bus', that the atmosphere suddenly changed, as a result of the German attack on Scandinavia. Set-backs to Allied arms in this area were deeply galling, for they implied an inferiority in naval warfare as well as in purely military

85

operations. A new Conservative 'cave' formed in opposition to Chamberlain, and in the great debate of early May the Labour Party decided to press a vote of censure. Chamberlain accepted the challenge defiantly but his majority sank to only eighty votes.

The invasion of the Low Countries and France was now taking place. The demands for a coalition were insistent, and Chamberlain asked Attlee whether the Labour Party would join the government, either under himself or under some other leader. Attlee referred the question to the National Executive, which was then attending the party conference at Bournemouth. The reply was that the party would take office only under another leader. This determined Chamberlain's fate and he resigned forthwith. A consultation then took place between Chamberlain, Halifax, and Churchill. It was agreed that Halifax was hardly suitable as Prime Minister owing to being in the Lords; and the post then fell to Churchill. Attlee discussed the new ministry with Churchill and agreed to a suggested allocation of the major offices. He then returned to Bournemouth to secure the party's confirmation of what he had done.

Attlee gave an account of his actions to meetings of the National Executive and the General Council of the T.U.C. After each had agreed unanimously with what he had done, an emergency resolution in this sense was moved at the following session of Conference. It was carried by an overwhelming vote. Thus Labour's acceptance of office was done in the most formal fashion, following procedure that was drawn up after the 1931 crisis, and taking advantage of the fact that Conference was in session. A new phase of the party's history was about to begin.

NOTES

1. Dalton, *Call Back Yesterday*, p. 277.
2. Harold Nicolson, *King George V* (1952), p. 491.
3. Report of meeting in T.U.C. file, quoted V. L. Allen, *Trade Unions and the Government* (1960), p. 258.

4. Lansbury to Bevin, March 1933, quoted Raymond Postgate, *Life of George Lansbury* (1951), p. 288.

5. *Labour Party Annual Report* (1934), p. 146.

6. Hugh Dalton, *The Fateful Years* (1957), p. 185.

7. C. R. Attlee, *As It Happened* (1954), p. 103.

FURTHER READING

The fullest narrative of party history in this period is to be found in G. D. H. Cole's *History of the Labour Party from 1914*. For interpretative comment, see R. W. Lyman, 'The Conflict between Socialist Ideals and Practical Politics between the Wars', *Journal of British Studies*, v (1965). Most of the biographies mentioned for the preceding period are also of importance for the 1930's, especially that of Bevin and the autobiographies of Citrine and Brockway. To these should be added John Campbell's *Nye Bevan* (1987), Raymond Postgate's *Life of George Lansbury* (1951), and Hugh Dalton, *The Fateful Years* (1957). Attlee's *As It Happened* (1954) is of value only to those who can read between the lines. His second volume, *A Prime Minister Remembers* (1961), is slightly more revealing and has now been supplemented by Kenneth Harris's authorised biography, *Attlee* (1982). Dean E. McHenry's *Labour Party in Transition, 1931–38* (1938) is a good contemporary analysis. J. F. Naylor, *Labour's International Policy* (1969) documents the contradictions of Labour foreign policy attitudes in this period, though not from original sources. Ben Pimlott, *Labour and the Left in the 1930s* (Cambridge, 1977) tells the story of the Socialist League and the United Front and provides interesting sketches of the party's leaders.

CHAPTER VI

Office and Power under Attlee and Bevin
(1940–50)

(1)

THE period of the 1940's includes both the full five years of the war-time Coalition and the only slightly shorter length of the 1945 Parliament, which provided for the first time a Labour Government with a Commons majority. Like the earlier periods which we have considered, this one has a certain unity about it, in spite of the great changes effected by the end of the war and by the general election. So far as the Labour Party was concerned, its parliamentary leaders were in office throughout, and gained power within the movement as a result. The extra-parliamentary party and the trade-union movement were consequently under constant restraint, sometimes critical of government policy but always anxious to avoid the embarrassment that would follow if they carried their protests beyond the limits of friendly admonishment.

The period thus formed a very marked contrast with the 1930's, when control of the movement was largely in the hands of the National Council of Labour, on which the General Council of the T.U.C. had a majority of seats. In 1940 the most powerful personality of the trade-union movement, Ernest Bevin, was brought in by Churchill to take office in the government; and the mutual understanding and affection that developed between him and Attlee provided the party with a stronger and more stable leadership than it had ever had before, even during the 1920's. Not that Attlee could establish the personal position that MacDonald had had, or could efface the memory of

Clement Attlee (1883-1967)

Ernest Bevin (1881-1951)

MacDonald within the party; but he and his colleagues knew that the only possible successor, if he gave up the leadership, was Bevin, and so long as he had Bevin's support he could ignore the occasional intrigues designed to force his resignation as leader, such as that voiced by Laski in 1945, or that in which Cripps took part in 1947. Instead, the degree of collaboration between Attlee and Bevin was remarkable for two men so different in their social origins and experience. As if to symbolise its loss of power, the National Council of Labour suffered a change of its constitution in 1941, whereby the Co-operative Union was brought in on an equal basis of representation with the T.U.C. and the Labour Party. Henceforward it was too clumsy an institution to have any real authority.

(2)

In proportion to its parliamentary strength in 1940, the Labour Party did very well indeed in the apportionment of offices made by Churchill as he became Prime Minister. There was to be a War Cabinet of five members, of whom two were to be Labour men — Attlee and Greenwood. In addition, Ernest Bevin became Minister of Labour and National Service, Herbert Morrison took the post of Minister of Supply, A. V. Alexander became First Lord of the Admiralty as in 1929, Hugh Dalton was Minister of Economic Warfare, and Sir William Jowitt was Solicitor-General. This large share of offices was partly the result of the party's role in the formation of the ministry and partly a recognition that at this time the Labour Party had a larger support in the country than it had in Parliament.

When Labour entered the government, some fresh arrangements had to be made for running the parliamentary party. The Parliamentary Executive therefore recommended, and the parliamentary party agreed to, the appointment of an Administrative Committee, consisting of members who were not ministers. While Attlee was to remain leader of the party, and with other ministers was to have access to meetings of the Administrative Committee, it was not expected that his attendance or that of other ministers would be very frequent. It was also agreed that the office of Leader of the Opposition should lapse for the duration of the Coalition. This meant that the salary of £2000 paid by the state to the Leader of the Opposition under the Ministers of the Crown Act, 1937, went into abeyance. Instead, H. B. Lees Smith, a senior Labour M.P. who had not been offered a post in the government, was chosen as Acting Chairman of the Parliamentary Party and hence became unofficial Leader of the Opposition. This arrangement was somewhat vexing to another prominent Labour member who had not taken office, Emanuel Shinwell. Shinwell had refused an appointment offered him by Churchill because he thought it unsuitable ; and he would have been a somewhat more effective Opposition leader than Lees Smith — in fact, rather too effective for the liking of the party as a whole.

As the war went on, changes took place in the government, but the rough balance of the parties was preserved. In September 1940 the War Cabinet was enlarged, and Bevin was brought in to make up a Labour group of three in a total of seven members. In October, Morrison was moved from Supply to the much more suitable post of Home Secretary and Minister of Home Security, where his knowledge of London government and personal popularity helped him much. In February 1941 Thomas Johnston became Secretary of State for Scotland. Then in February 1942 a more considerable reshuffle of government posts was made. Greenwood, who had not been a great success as a minister, relinquished office altogether ; but Cripps, who had been sent by Churchill as ambassador to Moscow, and who had come back with a somewhat unreal reputation as the man responsible for the improvement in Anglo-Soviet relations since the invasion of Russia, now entered the War Cabinet as Lord Privy Seal and Leader of the House of Commons — an extraordinary advance for one who had been ignominiously expelled from the Labour

Party for political extremism in 1939. Dalton moved to the Board of Trade and Attlee, while acknowledged now as Deputy Premier, also took the Dominions Office.

Cripps did not prove an entire success in his high office, and particularly as Leader of the House. Towards the end of the year, therefore, Churchill decided to move him to an administrative office outside the War Cabinet — that of Minister of Aircraft Production, admittedly a key post, and one in which his scientific training was of value. To restore the political balance, Morrison was brought into the War Cabinet, while retaining his post as Home Secretary and Minister of Home Security. Little further adjustment of responsibilities affecting the principal Labour ministers was made before 1945. The team was now working together well and the change in the fortunes of British arms removed one obvious incentive for change in the ministry.

The Coalition Government on the whole worked far more smoothly than that of the First World War. The very extremity of the crisis in 1940 made the Service chiefs more amenable to a single political control; the high reputation of Churchill as a strategist owed not a little to his length of experience and to the recognition that he almost alone had seen the need for urgent rearmament in the 1930's; and the readiness with which he could invigorate public opinion through B.B.C. broadcasts gave him a popular support which Lloyd George a quarter of a century earlier could only obtain by the grace of the press barons. At the same time, Churchill accepted the need for effective compromise between the political parties in the working out of domestic policy — a subject which really did not interest him very much while the war continued.

Much of the administration of home affairs during the war was conducted by Attlee. As the Prime Minister's deputy, he presided over Cabinets when Churchill was abroad; and as the need for high-level consultations with Allied leaders led Churchill to travel more frequently, Attlee's chairmanship became more and more practised. By contrast with Churchill's, Attlee's Cabinets disposed rapidly of the business that faced them: decisions were reached quickly instead of being postponed. All this not only widened Attlee's experience; it heightened his stature with his own colleagues, especially with Bevin, who had had little contact with him before 1940. The Labour ministers were also able to secure the passage of a limited amount of social legislation in the later part of the war. Prominent in this sphere were Thomas Johnston's hydro-electric scheme for the Scottish Highlands, Ernest Bevin's Catering Wages Act, and Dalton's Location of Industry Act, though the final stages of the latter were passed only after the end of the Coalition. It is true that little or no action was taken to implement a number of major commissions of enquiry which recommended reforms: this was notably the case with the Beveridge Report on Social Insurance, published in 1942 and taken up with much enthusiasm by the Press, but never officially approved of by the Coalition Government. Nevertheless, one very important change in the sphere of financial policy was accepted in 1944, when the principle of the need to secure full employment by government action was acknowledged in a White Paper. Attlee used this in a letter to Laski as a justification for the Labour Party's membership of the Coalition Government. 'The acceptance of these assumptions', he wrote, 'has its effect both in legislation and in administration, but its gradualness tends to hide our appreciation of the facts'.[1]

A subtle change came over the Coalition, however, as victory became imminent. Attlee tells us in his memoirs:

> I found . . . that it was more and more difficult to get post-war projects before the Cabinet. Agreements arrived at after long discussion by a Committee, on which both parties were fully represented, were blocked by the opposition of certain members of the Government who evinced a quite new interest in subjects hitherto outside the range of their attention.[2]

The ending of the war with Germany in May 1945 was of course the decisive turning-point. Thereafter, it was only a matter of jockeying for position by the two parties. Churchill, reckoning that his own great reputation would be of most value to the Conservatives immediately after the achievement of victory, suggested one of two alternatives to the Labour Party — either an immediate election or a continuation of the Coalition until the defeat of Japan. As the Labour Party Conference was meeting over Whitsun, Attlee was able to consult the National Executive as well as his immediate colleagues in the government in framing his reply. He suggested instead that the Coalition should continue until the autumn, which would give more time for the organisation of the campaign and the preparation of the list of voters.

Churchill, however, decided to yield to the pressure of his Conservative Party campaign advisers to hold the election as soon as practicable. Accordingly, the Labour Ministers handed in their seals of office later in May and the general election took place in July.

(3)

The general election of 1945 was on the whole a quiet one, conducted on an out-of-date register, albeit with a postal vote for the forces. The liveliest issue was that injected by Churchill, to the effect that if the Labour Party won the election, Attlee as Prime Minister would be under the control of Harold Laski, at that time Chairman of the National Executive. Some substance had been given to this possibility by Laski's own declaration that the Labour Party would not be bound by any commitments entered into by Attlee when, as the Leader of the Labour Party, he accompanied Churchill to the Potsdam Conference with Stalin and Truman in June. In a correspondence of increasing asperity, Churchill elaborated his charges on this score, while Attlee rebutted them, saying that 'at no time and in no circumstances has the National Executive Committee ever sought to give, or given, instructions to the Parliamentary Labour Party', and 'The Chairman has not the power to give me instructions'.

Naturally, nobody on the Labour Party side was disposed to challenge Attlee's arguments, and when it came to interpreting the Labour Party constitution Churchill was at a disadvantage. Consequently, Attlee got the better of these exchanges. All the same, Churchill was not unjustified in having doubts about the theoretical independence of a Labour Prime Minister, for, as we have seen, some efforts had been made in the 1930's to prevent the emergence of a new leader with as much power as Ramsay MacDonald had had, and the 1933 Conference had laid down a procedure for the Leader to follow in deciding whether to form a government, and how to choose his colleagues. But the matter was too little understood by the electorate to remove the impression that it was simply an election scare on the part of Churchill and his campaign advisers.

The election resulted in a dramatic victory for the Labour Party. Altogether 393 Labour M.P.s were returned, giving them a clear majority of 146 over all other parties It could not be said, however, that Labour had a clear majority among the voters: the Liberals still held the balance there, but on this occasion the bias present in the constituency system worked in favour of the Labour Party. It is doubtful if the party owed its success to its programme of reform, although this programme, comprising the nationalisation of several industries and promises of major social legislation, was very ably formulated by Herbert Morrison in the manifesto *Let Us Face the Future*. Rather than absorb these details, the electorate was probably voting as usual on the record of the past: the Conservatives had to take the blame for the Munich Agreement, and for the failure to rearm as well as for pre-war unemployment. There was also a good deal of concern lest the post-war situation should resemble that after the First World War, when the lavish promises of Lloyd George had led to very little fulfilment.

A striking feature of the results was that the trade-union-sponsored members of the new Parliamentary Labour Party were now less than a third of the total. The great change since the 1935 election was the flood of youngish middle-class Labour M.P.s, many of them professional men — lawyers, journalists, teachers, doctors, and dons. About two-thirds of the party had never been in Parliament before. This was in fact a new party, one that represented more fully than ever before all classes, all occupations, and all adult age-groups. The contrast with that first, highly homogeneous working-class party of 1906 was especially marked. Yet the natural internal discipline of the party was now immeasurably greater: so great in fact that it proved possible in June 1946 to suspend altogether the Standing Orders forbidding M.P.s to vote against party decisions.

When it came to forming a government, Attlee paid no attention to the procedure laid down by the 1933 Conference. As he later blandly put it in his memoirs, 'the passage of time and further experience has led to these proposals being tacitly dropped'.[3] In point of fact, however, there was a move by Herbert Morrison and others to delay Attlee's acceptance of the King's invitation to form a government until the parliamentary party had met and formally chosen its leader. Morrison claims in his own memoirs that he made this move solely in order to conform with the correct procedure, as formulated by Conference in the 1930's; and this is no doubt true.[4] In the event, however, he did not get his way, as both Attlee and Bevin were anxious to get on with the Cabinet-making. In any case, delay would only have appeared to confirm the truth of Churchill's charges made during the election.

Attlee decided to abandon the war-time system of having a small inner Cabinet. He sought instead a judiciously blended Cabinet of ministers without departments, available for the main Cabinet committee work, and ministers in charge of the main departments. The total came to nineteen. But there was a small group within the nineteen who had the responsibility of supervising whole fields of policy. These were Bevin, the Foreign Minister, who was concerned with all external matters including colonial policy; Herbert Morrison, the Lord President, who had to supervise the legislative programme and determine the order of nationalisation; Arthur Greenwood, the Lord Privy Seal, who in the early part of the war had instructed Beveridge to draw up his famous report, and who was now in charge of the social services; and Hugh Dalton, the Chancellor of the Exchequer, whose office naturally entailed great influence.

Within this inner ring, Attlee retained personal authority of no mean order. Bevin was his closest confidant: yet in making his Cabinet he exchanged the proposed offices of Bevin and Dalton, at first disappointing both men; and Morrison, although claiming that this change was made at his own suggestion, admits that he himself had little intimacy with Attlee: 'It was quite impossible to approach near enough . . . to know what he was really thinking.'[5] Nor can Greenwood have been any more in Attlee's confidence: at any rate, Attlee had no hesitation in dismissing him from office in 1947 on the grounds that, at the age of 68, he was too old. This would not have been so bad for Greenwood if Attlee had not replaced him with Lord Addison, who was ten years older. In the sphere of defence, Attlee at first followed Churchill's example by himself acting as the Minister of Defence, but in 1946 he appointed A. V. Alexander to this office, at the same time excluding the heads of the three services from membership of the Cabinet.

The legislative programme of nationalisation went through Parliament with remarkable smoothness. First of all came the measure nationalising the Bank of England, which met with little opposition from the Conservatives, Churchill himself saying that it 'does not, in my opinion, raise any matter of principle'.[6] Then came the establishment of the National Coal Board, a public but semi-independent body, having a limited responsibility to the Minister of Fuel and Power. Here again there was little spirited opposition to the take-over of what was clearly a very inefficient industry. Rather more controversy was aroused, however, by the establishment of the British Transport Commission in 1947, not so much because it took over the railways and canals, which had already been very unprofitable, as because it also included the road haulage business. It was as a result of this legislation that British Road Services came into existence. The nationalisation of cable and wireless companies and the establishment of public corporations to run the airlines merely continued a policy accepted by earlier governments. In 1948 and 1949 respectively the British Electricity Authority and the Gas Council were set up to take over management of two further public utilities, both of which were already under substantial public control.

The most vigorous political controversy in respect of nationalisation took place over the iron and steel industry. This was deliberately left to the last by the government because of the difficulties ^f defining how far the nationalisation should go and what the new form of the industry should be. Iron and steel is a very complex industry in which ownership overlaps substantially into engineering and other industries. Furthermore, at the time it was both profitable and comparatively efficient. These considerations led to the Prime Minister secretly sponsoring an enquiry, carried out by Herbert Morrison, into the possibility of the industry accepting a Board of Control appointed by the government, in return for the abandonment of nationalisation. Morrison was able to report a wide measure of agreement for the proposal, but it was hotly opposed in Cabinet by Bevan and others, and was therefore abandoned.[7] To allow further time for the preparation of the measure, an act was passed reducing the delaying power of the House of Lords from two years to one. In 1949 an act was passed to enable the government to purchase the assets of the iron and steel companies, without completely altering the industry's structure. The Lords in fact agreed to this act after persuading the government to postpone the date of its operation until after the forthcoming general election.

Thus the Labour Party's 1945 proposals for nationalisation were all carried out, so far as legislation was concerned, before the end of the Parliament. If they all came into operation, some 20 per cent of the economy, it was estimated, would be in public ownership. Yet, as so often happens, the changes of the period which had the greatest impact on everyday social life were budgetary rather than purely legislative. And in this sphere the government faced the problem not only of redistributing the nation's wealth but also of increasing it so that Britain could pay her way in the world's markets. After the sudden end of American Lend-Lease in 1945, a large dollar loan was negotiated, but the money was spent unexpectedly quickly and a major foreign exchange crisis occured in 1947. An emergency programme for expanding exports had to be devised, and for this purpose Sir Stafford Cripps was made Minister for Economic Affairs. Dalton, the Chancellor, prepared an autumn budget but an indiscretion to a journalist deprived him of office and enabled Cripps to combine the two posts.

Cripps now exercised a wide control over the economic affairs of the nation, and became the most influential person in the government after Attlee and Bevin. He imposed a programme of 'austerity' — heavy taxation on internal consumption and the restriction of overseas purchases and foreign travel, so as to enable the deficit in the country's foreign exchange account to be made up. The unions were persuaded to accept a policy of 'wage restraint' so as to keep down costs and enable British exports to compete effectively abroad. They agreed to this the more willingly because Cripps retained the highly redistributive taxation system which had operated during the war and kept a strict control on the price level.

So far as general popularity was concerned, the most acceptable measures of the Labour Government were in the sphere of the social services. The school leaving age was raised to fifteen, and state scholarships to the universities were increased. The Beveridge social insurance proposals were implemented by the enactment of James Griffiths' National Insurance Act, and Aneurin Bevan as Minister of Health introduced the National Health Service, which provided free medical treatment and free drugs, and which involved the nationalisation of the hospitals. Bevan was less successful in dealing with housing, however, for although he encouraged construction by local authorities for cheap letting, and kept a tight rein on private building, he did not achieve the target of two hundred thousand houses annually which the government had promised.

By far the most contentious areas of policy within the Labour Party itself were foreign affairs and defence. Bevin, as Foreign Secretary, soon found that he was faced by an unexpectedly intransigent attitude on the part of the Russian Government. Realising the economic weakness not only of Britain but also of the rest of Europe, Bevin therefore worked for effective collaboration with the United States. He did much to bring the 'Marshall Plan' into existence, which had a powerfully invigorating effect in stimulating recovery throughout Western Europe; and he was a prime mover in creating the North Atlantic Treaty Organisation. This policy of association with the United States and of re-armament to resist Russian pressure did not commend itself very warmly to the rank and file of the Labour Party. The concept of a 'Socialist' foreign policy, it was felt, had been abandoned: at the very least, an attempt should have been made to retain a position of independence between the capitalist and the Communist world — if possible, to form a bridge between them.

The Labour critics of the government's foreign policy really fell into three categories. There were, first of all, the out-and-out pacifists who, like Lansbury before the war, preferred the entire abandonment of all military preparation; secondly, there was a small band of crypto-Communists, including a group of four or five Labour M.P.s and the officials of a number of unions controlled by the extreme Left, who could see nothing wrong in Russian foreign policy; and thirdly, there was a larger body of opinion, strong in the parliamentary party and focused in the 'Keep Left' group of M.P.s, who advocated the creation of a 'third force' of powers between Russia and America, and led by Britain. The 'Keep Left' group moved an amendment

99

to the King's Speech in November 1946, but did not carry it to a vote. The policy, unfortunately, suffered from two defects: it took no account of the increasing tendency of political regimes outside the Communist sphere to swing in the direction of greater Conservatism; and it ignored the economic dependence of Britain and of other non-Communist powers upon the United States.

In the sphere of defence a revolt of seventy-two Labour M.P.s in April 1947 led to a rather undignified reversal of government policy, whereby the length of military service was cut from eighteen months to twelve. This appeared to be a victory for the Left: but an attempt to force the foreign policy issue at the Labour Party Conference of 1947 was easily defeated by Bevin. Speaking of the King's Speech amendment moved by the 'Keep Left' group, he described himself as having been 'stabbed in the back' by it, and added rather pointedly, 'I grew up in the trade union, you see, and I have never been used to this kind of thing'.[8] No card vote was called for after his speech, for it was obvious that he could rely upon the big battalions of the trade-union vote. After this, the 'Keep Left' revolt was virtually at an end. Only the pacifists and the crypto-Communists kept up their attacks, and continued to cause embarrassment to the government. The attitude of the pacifists was of course understandable, and had always been covered by the 'conscience clause' of Standing Orders; but the crypto-Communists were in a different case, and eventually they were all expelled from the party. They set up their own little party of 'Labour Independents' in the House. All of them were defeated in the 1950 election.

It remains to say a word about what will probably rank as the most important field of government policy — namely, the creation of the new states in Asia. Attlee, who had served on the Simon Commission for India, acted decisively by fixing a time-limit for the withdrawal of British troops from India, and he sent Lord Mountbatten as the last Viceroy to accomplish the transfer of power. In 1947, therefore, two new nations were created, India and Pakistan. Burma and Ceylon also achieved their independence. Yet of these four new states only Burma chose to sever its links with the Commonwealth. The situation in Palestine was less well handled, largely owing to the desire to keep on good terms with the Arab countries; and the withdrawal of British troops in 1948 was followed by a period of warfare between Jews and Arabs which ended in the establishment of the independent state of Israel.

(4)

The steady support of the labour movement outside Parliament for the work of the government was largely due to the trade-union leadership of the period. Bevin's position in the government was one of complete loyalty to Attlee, and his own record in the unions in turn guaranteed the government as a whole the fidelity of the major unions including his own Transport and General Workers, now ruled by his former assistant Arthur Deakin. The only real danger lay in the possibility that Communist infiltration of key posts in major unions might suddenly result in a change of policy. The danger became fully apparent after the alteration in the Communist 'line' in 1947, when in response to the initiative of the newly-founded 'Cominform' British Communists began to regard Attlee and Bevin as 'loyal supporters of the imperialists'.[9] Arthur Deakin and others then became seriously alarmed at the extent of Communist penetration of the unions; and accordingly the General Council of the T.U.C. issued a warning to the unions. In 1949 Deakin persuaded his own union to accept a rule preventing Communists from holding office; and this led to the dismissal of nine full-time officials at the end of the year. No such measure was possible in the Mineworkers or in the Engineers, which were both rather decentralised unions with strong existing pockets of Communist control. But in the Mineworkers the issue took the form of a stern disciplining of the Communist secretary, Arthur

Horner, by the President, Will Lawther, who had the executive on his side. In the General and Municipal Workers Union, the largest of the other unions, a rule banning Communists had been in operation ever since the 1920's. The Electrical Trades Union and the Fire Brigades Union, together with one or two smaller unions, were already wholly or largely under Communist control, but they did not constitute a very large voting element at party conferences. Under these circumstances, the unions gave their support to the government and accepted the policy of wage restraint — a policy unique in union history and inevitably dangerous for union officials to pursue for very long without risking the loss of their popularity with their members.

The collapse of the 'Keep Left' movement and the absorption of the party in the accomplishment of the legislative programme prevented any major open discords from damaging the party's chances at the impending general election. Cabinet differences there had been, particularly over iron and steel, but these had been largely hidden from the public. And, as we have seen, Attlee's position, with the support of Bevin, was unassailable. One remarkable achievement of the party in the period from 1945 to 1950 was that it had not lost a single seat at a by-election. At the beginning of 1950 the party prepared to stand upon its record, and indeed it had had little opportunity to work out a further detailed programme of nationalisation. The policy statement for the election, *Labour Believes in Britain*, which was again largely drawn up by Morrison, mentioned only sugar, cement, and water supply as industries suitable for public ownership within the period of the next Parliament.

Undoubtedly a swing against Labour was to be expected. The 'austerity' of the preceding years and the continuation of many shortages and many forms of rationing were naturally unpopular, and the government got the blame. Conservative party organisation was enormously better than in 1945, while the Labour party organisation had improved comparatively little. Furthermore, although the Representation of the People Act of 1948 abolished the university seats and the business vote, the advantage that the Labour Party thereby gained was more than offset by the redistribution of seats necessary to take account of population movement. The electoral system in the 1950's in fact had a slight 'bias' against the Labour Party, accounted for by the fact that the party's support in some exclusively working-class areas was so solid and uniform that it provided enormous Labour majorities, while the Conservative vote was less highly concentrated in a few constituencies and so more effective. It was calculated after the 1950 election, for instance, that with the Liberal vote at its existing level, the Conservative Party needed only 44·5 per cent of the total vote for its candidates in order to win a clear majority in the Commons, while Labour needed 46·5 per cent.[10] In the actual results, the Labour Party secured over 13¼ million votes — three-quarters of a million more than the Conservatives and 46·8 per cent of the total where it put up candidates. This gave it a very slight majority in the House: 315 seats, as against 298 for the Conservatives, 9 Liberals, and 2 Irish Nationalists. The closeness of the contest and the abolition of the university seats helped to eliminate the independents; but the general verdict of the electorate could hardly be regarded as a decisive one. The working-class vote in favour of the Labour Party — never of course a complete one — had changed little, but there seemed to be a considerable defection of middle-class voters, for many seats in suburban London and the Home Counties reverted to Conservative allegiance. The overall swing from Labour to Conservative, if compared with 1945, was 3·3 per cent; but in Wales it was only ·3 per cent, and in some parts of rural England it was less than 1 per cent.

According to Morrison, Attlee would have done better to delay the election from February, when it actually took place, to June: the Labour voters were always put off by bad weather, but would respond better in the warmer and lighter days of summer. Since the result was so close, there may have been something in this argument, but Attlee of course did not know beforehand what accidental misfortune might make things difficult for the party later in the year. At any rate, the result of the 1950 election closed a period of the party's history : it deprived it of its effective control of the legislature and began the decline in its parliamentary fortunes which continued for an entire decade.

NOTES

1. Attlee to Laski, 1 May 1944, quoted Kingsley Martin, *Harold Laski* (1953), p. 161.
2. C. R. Attlee, *As It Happened* (1954), p. 132.
3. Attlee, *op. cit.* p. 156.
4. Herbert Morrison, *Autobiography* (1960), p. 245.
5. *Ibid.* p. 295.
6. Hansard, *Parliamentary Debates*, ser. 5, ccccxiii, 94.
7. Morrison, *op. cit.* p. 296.
8. *Labour Party Annual Report* (1947), p. 179.
9. *World News and Views*, xxvii (1947), 463 f.
10. These figures and those that follow are taken from H. G. Nicholas, *British General Election of 1950* (1951).

FURTHER READING

For the years of the Coalition we are largely dependent upon volumes of memoirs, notably those by Attlee and Dalton which have already been mentioned, to which Emanuel Shinwell, *Conflict Without Malice* (1955), and Herbert Morrison, *Autobiography* (1960), should be added. John Campbell's *Nye Bevan* is an important contribution; and there are some interesting letters published in Kingsley Martin, *Harold Laski.* On Labour's role in the Coalition, see T. D. Burridge, *British Labour & Hitler's War* (1976) and S. Brooke, *Labour's War* (Oxford, 1992). On the period of the Labour Government, there are now two critical studies, K. O. Morgan, *Labour in Power, 1945–51* (1984) and Henry Pelling, *The Labour Governments, 1945–51* (1984). The authoritative study of Labour foreign policy is Alan Bullock, *Ernest Bevin: Foreign Secretary* (1983).

There are also some valuable works of political analysis. Robert T. McKenzie's *British Political Parties* (new ed., 1963) is useful for this period, and we also have the Nuffield election studies, starting with R. B. McCallum and A. Redman, *British General Election of 1945* (1947), and followed by H. G. Nicholas's volume for 1950. Two volumes dealing with the political links of the trade unions must also be mentioned: Martin Harrison, *Trade Unions and the Labour Party since 1945* (1960), and V. L. Allen, *Trade Unions and the Government* (1960).

CHAPTER VII

Dissension and Decline
(*1950–60*)

(1)

THE main characteristics of the 1950's for the Labour Party were : public dissension among its leaders, and a decline of its popularity with the electorate. The two features were of course connected, though perhaps not as closely as some people may imagine, for, as we have seen, there had been plenty of open disagreements within the party in its long years of growth before the Second World War.

In the course of the decade the parliamentary leadership ceased to dominate the party as it had done in the 1940's. Attlee, of course, until his retirement in 1955, retained great prestige as the past and possible future Prime Minister ; but he was getting on in years (his seventieth birthday was in January 1953), and the great bulwark of his power in the party, Ernest Bevin, had been removed by death in 1951. On the other hand, the dissident Left, led by Aneurin Bevan, won much support among the active members of the constituency parties ; and as a result the National Executive, which was an important focus of power in the party when it was not in office, became a cockpit of conflict. Constitutionally, the Executive's functions were supposed to be in the sphere of administration rather than of policy, but the distinction had never been maintained in practice.

At first, it is true, the ultimate power in Conference seemed to remain in the hands of the major trade-union leaders, of whom the most important was Arthur Deakin, Bevin's successor as secretary of the Transport and General

Workers. It was largely Deakin and his colleagues Will Lawther of the Mineworkers and Tom Williamson of the General and Municipal Workers who in 1955 determined the succession to the party leadership. But Deakin died before his purpose was finally accomplished, and a few months later his own office as secretary of the Transport Workers fell to a left-wing militant, Frank Cousins — an event that immensely weakened the block of right-wing trade-union leaders in the party. Bevin and Deakin in their turn had been king-makers: Cousins so far had been no more than a *frondeur*. All the same, by 1960 the *fronde* had gone so far that the attempt of the party leader himself to take the initiative in shaping the party's destinies — most notably, by the revision of Clause Four of the constitution — resulted only in a face-saving compromise which suggested that positive leadership was temporarily impracticable.

(2)

The general election of February 1950 had given the Labour Party an overall Commons majority of only six, and this created a parliamentary situation that made government almost impossible. It was quite out of the question to attempt any contentious legislation, and the ordinary needs of administration could only be satisfied by great strain upon both ministers and M.P.s — for, however busy or ill they were, they were obliged to attend all important divisions in the House so as to save the government from premature defeat. Much to the fury of the Conservatives, the government allowed the nationalisation of iron and steel to take effect in February 1951. This could be done under the act which had passed on to the statute book in 1949.

Many of the government's difficulties, however, were caused by troubles within its own ranks. Several of its senior members were suffering from ill-health, and two of them, Bevin and Cripps, were forced to resign for that reason and shortly afterwards died. Cripps gave up the

Exchequer in October 1950, being succeeded by Hugh Gaitskell, now aged 44, who had proved his value as an efficient administrator in junior posts; Bevin resigned the Foreign Office in February 1951 and was replaced by Herbert Morrison. The Prime Minister himself went into hospital at Easter, 1951, and almost immediately, without the steadying influence of the older leaders, dissensions began in the Cabinet. Faced by the heavy costs of the rearmament programme, which had been necessitated by the Korean War, Gaitskell in his budget decided to put charges upon the supply of dentures and spectacles under the National Health Service. This provoked the resignation in April 1951 of Bevan, who was now Minister of Labour, of Harold Wilson, who was President of the Board of Trade, and of John Freeman, Parliamentary Secretary to the Ministry of Supply.

Meanwhile, the government was still losing what popularity it had in the country. One cause of this was Morrison's handling of a dispute with Persia, which resulted in the expulsion of the staff of the Anglo-Iranian Oil Company by the Persian Government. Probably no stronger policy was practicable, especially in the absence of a mobile striking force; but, in any case, Morrison was not experienced either in the conduct of foreign policy or in the art of explaining it to the country, as Bevin had been. Even more important, so far as the electorate was concerned, was the inflationary strain on the economy caused by the impact of the Korean War and the resulting rise in raw material and transport costs. The official index of prices, which in February 1950 stood at 113, rose rapidly in 1951 to a figure of 129 in October.

It was at this point that Attlee held a new election, probably with little hope of improving the Labour Party's position, but at least with the expectation that, one way or the other, stronger government would be assured. Naturally, the election, coming so soon after the very close result of 1950, was regarded as a renewed contest between the two major parties; and so the Liberals and the candidates of smaller parties or the independents stood very little chance of election. Consequently the number of candidates was much smaller than in 1950. The main issues of the campaign were the cost of living and the danger of war: the Conservatives concentrated on the former, the Labour Party on the latter. According to Conservative speakers, Labour administration had led to a rapid devaluation of the pound; and Anthony Eden made a television broadcast on this theme, using a chart which was later strongly criticised on technical grounds by Labour. The Labour Party, for its part, maintained that the Conservative attitude on the Persian question showed that they were 'warmongers': the *Daily Mirror*, which was supporting Labour, came out with an election-day front page asking 'Whose Finger on the Trigger?'

In spite of its disadvantages the Labour Party secured the highest total poll that it or any other party has received up to the present day in a British general election: about fourteen million votes. The Conservatives received about a quarter of a million less, and yet won a majority of the seats. This was owing to the natural bias of the electoral system already mentioned. The new House therefore had 321 Conservative M.P.s, 295 Labour, 6 Liberals, and 3 Irish Independents. The Conservatives thus had an overall majority of 17 — a small figure, but two and a half times as large as that of Labour in 1950. The change of government was effected by a national swing of only 1·1 per cent of the voters — a swing, however, which was so remarkably uniform over the whole country as to cause rather too firm generalisations to be made about the homogeneity of the electorate. It must be remembered that regional and local variations in electoral behaviour always tend to be obscured if elections are held at such short intervals as that between February 1950 and October 1951.

On the whole, the Labour Party could regard these results with a reasonable degree of satisfaction. After all, it was no bad thing for a party exhausted by the tasks of administration to regroup itself in opposition, especially after an election which gave its opponents such a small majority and such a disappointing mandate. The danger was, however, that satisfaction would easily degenerate into complacency; and in the succeeding years the party paid all too little attention to the business of winning future elections. Instead, controversy within the ranks, already launched when Labour was in power, came to dominate its activities, absorbing much of the energies of the members; and party organisation, both at the centre and at the local level, suffered in consequence.

(3)

In March 1952 the conflict between the Bevanites, as the minority were called, and the parliamentary leadership came out into the open in a Commons debate on rearmament. Attlee and his colleagues had decided to move an amendment to the government motion on defence, but not to oppose the motion itself. Fifty-seven Labour M.P.s, however, did vote against the motion — a group which was later called 'the 57 varieties' because it contained a mixture of people with different motives — not only Bevan and his colleagues who had resigned from the government, but also the remnant of the old 'Keep Left' group including of course the pacifists. The revolt was less serious than it might seem, for Standing Orders, which had been suspended in 1946, had still not been reimposed, and so there was no formal breach of party discipline. But the result was the reimposition of Standing Orders, by decision of the parliamentary party, before the month was out. This meant that the parliamentary minority would be unable to express its views freely in the lobbies, and henceforward the battle would have to be fought outside Parliament. Anyone who voted contrary to the decision of the parliamentary party would risk expulsion and that, as was shown by the fate of independent candidates at recent general elections, would almost inevitably mean losing one's seat at the next contest.

Bevan's supporters in the parliamentary party were mostly nominees of the constituency parties, rather than of the trade unions; many of them were professional men, especially journalists. The leaders of the group, such as Michael Foot, Tom Driberg, and Richard Crossman, were active political columnists with plenty of opportunity to publicise their views and to try to win support. In *Tribune* they had their own political organ, and they could also make substantial use of the *New Statesman*. Neither of these weeklies was widely read by trade unionists, but both were much favoured by the constituency party rank and file. All the same, by far the greatest asset of the Bevanites was Bevan's own strong personality and his exceptional oratorical capacity.

The first major extra-parliamentary conflict came at the 1952 party conference. To the indignation of the leading union officials, no less than six of the seven constituency party seats on the Executive were won by the Bevanites, and both Morrison and Dalton were displaced. As it happened, Arthur Deakin was due to speak as fraternal delegate from the T.U.C., and he took the opportunity to demand the dissolution of the *Tribune* group, threatening the formation of counter-organisation if it continued. This apparently had its effect upon Attlee, for when the parliamentary party met later in the month, he demanded 'the immediate abandonment of all group organisation within the party other than those officially recognised'.[1] A resolution to this effect was carried by 188 votes to 51. Fifty-three M.P.s did not vote, owing to either absence or abstention. It was significant, however, that when in the following month the elections for the offices of the parliamentary party were held, Bevan obtained 82 votes against Morrison's 194 for the Deputy Leadership. Yet Bevan was the only one of his group to be elected to the Parliamentary Committee or 'shadow cabinet'.

By this time Attlee was almost seventy and was showing signs of tiredness. The question of succession had to be considered, and yet Morrison, who was the obvious claimant in many ways, had just suffered the ignominy of being thrown off the National Executive. The right-wing union leaders — Deakin, Lawther, and Williamson, who between them could guarantee about a third of the conference vote — offered Morrison their support for the Treasurership at the 1953 conference if he would stand against the ailing Greenwood, who had held the post since 1943. Morrison at first accepted, but when the conference was already in session he realised the strength of sentiment in favour of Greenwood, a respected incumbent in what was after all largely a sinecure. Morrison therefore withdrew, accepting a compromise whereby the Deputy Leader was given an *ex officio* place on the Executive. Morrison's chances of succeeding to the party leadership were not lost, but they were undoubtedly damaged by this manœuvre.

It was at this point that a fresh issue arose to divide the party and to give the Bevanites their greatest opportunity — the issue of German rearmament. The Churchill government had been persuaded by the Americans to accept the principle, but it was natural that the Opposition should have more difficulty in agreeing. After a discussion in the Parliamentary Labour Party, with Attlee and Morrison both urging acceptance, a favourable vote was carried by the small margin of 113 to 104. The issue came more fully into the open in April 1954, when Bevan resigned from the 'shadow cabinet', ostensibly because he was dissatisfied with the party's attitude on Far Eastern policy, but actually so as to take the lead in a campaign to reverse the decision over German rearmament at the forthcoming party conference. This action was likely to prejudice the party at the next election, which could not now be far in the future; and Harold Wilson, although nominally a Bevanite, consequently decided to accept the place in the 'shadow cabinet' which had been vacated by Bevan and for which, as it happened, he (Wilson) had been the runner-up in the parliamentary party's elections.

There were two main issues of conflict at the party's 1954 conference. One of them was the succession to the

Treasurership, now vacant owing to the death of Green-wood; the other was the issue of German rearmament. Morrison could not contest the Treasurership, now that he was on the Executive as Deputy Leader; and the trade-union leadership therefore put up Gaitskell as a rival to their enemy Bevan. Gaitskell had won the respect of the miners both because of his early work among them as a W.E.A. lecturer and more recently as Minister of Fuel. He now gained the support of Arthur Deakin and the other right-wing union leaders. As a result, he won, by over four million votes to Bevan's two million. It was not quite so easy, however, to put Bevan in the minority over German rearmament. This was a matter on which the rank and file of the party was deeply stirred, and it brought the Left a good deal of support which it could not normally expect. At the same time, this vote coming shortly before a general election would obviously be binding on the party, and thus it was a vital test for the leadership of Attlee and Morrison. In the upshot, the leadership was upheld by a majority of only a quarter of a million votes out of a total of six million. The decision was determined only by a last-minute switch on the part of the delegates of the Woodworkers and a few smaller unions which followed their lead.

Both decisions were galling for those who disliked the use of the unions' block vote, and not least so for the Bevan-ites and Bevan himself. He determined to continue his campaign to convert the party, and especially to try to win a foothold among the unions. At a meeting organised by *Tribune* before the conference was over he felt free to speak out about the decisions made, and it was on this occasion that he referred to Gaitskell — admittedly not very explicitly — as 'a desiccated calculating machine'. In point of fact, however, Gaitskell's capacity as an orator was steadily improving, and he proved able to hold his own on the platform of the party conference without any difficulty.

As the next election grew more and more imminent, so did the need for party unity increase. Yet early in 1955 Bevan gave yet another public parade of insubordination to the parliamentary leadership. It is true that the issue involved was one in which conscientious scruples were quite justified : the manufacture and use of the hydrogen bomb. The British Government's decision to make the bomb was announced in the Defence White Paper of 1955, and Bevan and his followers felt that this should not be accepted without some definite restrictions upon its use. The Bevanite group therefore expressed dissatisfaction with the official Opposition amendment to the motion approving the White Paper, and decided to abstain from voting. Altogether, a total of sixty-two Labour M.P.s abstained from the vote in this way : a gesture that was rather humiliating to the party leadership but which did not technically offend against Standing Orders, as abstention on grounds of conscience was permitted. But Bevan compounded his offence by interrupting Attlee's speech during the debate and putting a question to him. The 'shadow cabinet', under pressure from Morrison, therefore decided to withdraw the whip from Bevan, and this decision was rather reluctantly confirmed by the parliamentary party by a majority of 141 votes to 112.

It was clear that Morrison and the major trade-union leaders were anxious to have done with Bevan by expelling him from the party altogether. In particular, Arthur Deakin was active in lobbying members of the National Executive to secure this end. There were, however, many M.P.s and others who, while not agreeing with Bevan's views, felt that his expulsion would prove very damaging to the party. In the end, a compromise was proposed by Attlee on the National Executive and carried by 14 to 13. This enabled Bevan to retain his membership of the party after making an apology for his behaviour. An earlier initiative by Attlee might well have prevented the matter from being so fiercely debated : as always, he played a waiting game to the last moment — as Morrison put it, he 'doodled when he ought to have led'.[2] This, however, was the method by which Attlee had preserved his own position for so many years.

Only two weeks after this meeting of the National Executive, Churchill resigned from the Premiership, to be succeeded by Eden. Almost immediately the new Prime Minister decided on a general election, and this took place in May. The moment was a good one for the Conservatives, not only because of the controversy within the Labour Party, but because of the economic recovery of the time, which had enabled Butler as Chancellor of the Exchequer to make a number of tax cuts. Butler's budgets, not so very different from Gaitskell's when he had been Chancellor, had led to the coining of the word 'Butskellite' to describe the cautious and uncontroversial policy that both had pursued. Though the word was often used with opprobrium, the policy seemed on the whole to be popular, and it deprived the Labour Party of effective weapons of criticism. At the same time, the Labour Party suffered owing to its links with the unions, which were unpopular in the early summer of 1955 because of a number of strikes, each affecting a wide public. A newspaper strike, lasting almost a month, was followed during the election period by a dock strike and the threat of a rail strike: and both these latter disputes arose not out of direct conflict with employers but through inter-union rivalries.

The election was on the whole a quiet one. Both parties concentrated on the need for high-level meetings to secure peace, and the Labour Party failed to win any enthusiasm for its nationalisation proposals, which again comprehended steel and road haulage and added in 'sections of the chemical and machine-tool industries'. The electors were apathetic, meetings were generally small, partly, but only partly, owing to the use of television as a political medium; and the Labour Party machine in particular was shown to be very rusty. Internal dissensions had weakened the party's efficiency, and it was significant that the number of full-time agents in the constituencies had dropped from 296 in 1951 to only 227. The Conservative Party, on the other hand, seemed as efficient as before. The result was that the Conservatives increased their parliamentary majority over all other parties from 17 in 1951 to 58. This was the first time for almost a century that a government had managed to increase its majority at a general election. The Labour Party's share of the poll dropped from 48·8 to 46·4 per cent, and was now less than the Conservative share by over 3 per cent. The swing from Labour to Conservative was about 1·8 per cent, but this time it was somewhat uneven in different parts of the country : it was substantially less in Scotland, perhaps owing to unemployment there, and substantially more in the Midlands where prosperity was greater. In East Anglia there was actually a slight swing to Labour : this was apparently due to the progress of the National Union of Agricultural Workers among the farm labourers there. The Conservatives now had a total of 344 M.P.s, while Labour had 277 ; the Liberals had 6 again and the Sinn Fein had 2.

Owing to the general apathy even the Conservative poll was down by some 400,000 compared with 1951 ; but the Labour poll had fallen by over 1½ million. Naturally enough, therefore, the Labour leaders drew the conclusion that their failure had been caused by the abstention of Labour voters, due to the party's internal differences and the weakness of its organisation. The National Executive immediately appointed a sub-committee under the chairmanship of Harold Wilson to enquire into the state of party organisation and report to the next party conference in October 1955. The committee found that many of the difficulties were beyond the control of the party : for instance, there had been a shortage of voluntary workers which had been due at least in part to full employment, overtime, and the employment of married women. But there were also serious faults in the work of full-time employees of the party and in the use of the party's funds. The report recommended the creation of a special sub-committee of the National Executive to supervise the work of organisation ; special help in future for marginal constituencies ; and a decentralisation of organisation to regional offices. An illustration of the poverty of the existing structure

was given in the comment made in the report : 'We recommend that the necessary steps be taken to enable members
of the Regional Staff to buy cars for use on organisation
work'.[3]

(4)

All these matters should of course have been attended
to in the years after the 1951 election, and one reason why
they were not attended to, apart from the controversies
within the party, was that the principal leaders were getting
old and losing touch with the necessities of the new era.
The recognition of this fact came soon after the 1955 defeat,
and not only Attlee but also many of his colleagues gave
up the positions of authority which they had so long held,
in order to make way for younger men.

The fact that Attlee himself had clung to the leadership
of the party for so long had encouraged others to stay with
him in the 'shadow cabinet'. Attlee's motives have been
subjected to some speculation : it may have been that he
for his part wished to outlast Winston Churchill, who was
more than eight years older than himself. Or it may have
been that he recognised the difficulty of handing over to
Morrison, when Morrison was both likely to widen the
breach with the Bevanites and unable to secure the support
of the constituency parties. But in any case, Attlee could
hardly carry on much beyond the 1955 election.

When the new parliament assembled, Dalton, who had
always been anxious to encourage the younger members of
the party, decided that the time was ripe for his own resignation and for that of as many as possible of his elderly colleagues. He clearly wished to open the way to the leadership
for his former protégé, Hugh Gaitskell. He therefore wrote
to Attlee announcing his own retirement on grounds of age,
and pointing out that no less than nine members of the
'shadow cabinet' were already over 65. He urged Attlee's
retention of office 'in the interests of party unity', but was
simultaneously putting pressure on his other colleagues to
retire. In fact, four of them did so — among them being

Emanuel Shinwell and William Whiteley (the Chief Whip). Morrison remained, but he was now 67, and Dalton's remarks had built up an atmosphere of doubt about his capacity for high office in the future.

Meanwhile Gaitskell's ability as a parliamentary spokesman of the party became more and more obvious. It was this, together with the feeling that Morrison's best years were over, that swung the trade-union M.P.s to his support. Consequently, when Attlee at last resigned the leadership at the end of 1955, sentiment had crystallised in Gaitskell's favour and he was elected leader of the party by a substantial majority. The figures were : Gaitskell, 157 ; Bevan, 70 ; Morrison, 40. Morrison was taken aback by this result and refused to act as Deputy Leader ; the old middle-of-the-road stalwart James Griffiths was elected in his place. It was noteworthy, however, that Bevan, also standing for the Deputy Leadership, secured 111 votes against 141 for Griffiths : as Griffiths was the older man, this clearly suggested that if Bevan wanted to take the Deputy Leadership at some future date, he would be able to do so unless factional strife broke out once more.

It might be supposed that the election of Gaitskell, who had been considered more right-wing than Attlee, would be the signal for a fresh outburst of factional strife. But as was shown at the 1956 conference, the older right-wing block of trade-union votes had begun to disintegrate of its own accord. Bevan stood again for the Treasurership and this time won, securing the support of both the Mineworkers and the Railwaymen as well as of the constituency parties. The election of Frank Cousins, a left-wing militant, as secretary of the Transport and General Workers, the largest single voting unit in the conference, completed the picture of disarray on the right wing of the party.

Shortly afterwards there occurred the government's disastrous Suez operation, which solidified the Labour Party behind its leadership and revived, at least momentarily, the early prospect of a return to power. The government's policy was hotly debated both in Parliament and outside, and Gaitskell and Bevan in particular worked well together, both of them making effective fighting speeches. The National Council of Labour suddenly re-awoke to launch a popular campaign under the slogan 'Law not War'. Support for this came from people of all parties, especially intellectuals: and for a brief moment it was like the 1930's over again.

After the dust had begun to settle a little, in early 1957, it became clear that the Suez affair had both united the Labour Party and strengthened it in the constituencies. Gaitskell now felt able to give Bevan the post of 'shadow foreign secretary' which he had desired; and the results of the by-elections showed the unpopularity of the government, which redounded to the advantage of Labour and Liberals alike. It was not so much that opposition to the Suez campaign had been general in the country — on the contrary, there was a strong feeling of popular jingoism which was evident even among regular Labour supporters — but rather that the increase in petrol prices and other temporary results of the failure of the campaign lowered the standing of the government.

It was the Labour Party's misfortune, however, that the collapse of Sir Anthony Eden placed a really formidable opponent, Harold Macmillan, in the office of Prime Minister. Combining to a remarkable degree the qualities of intelligence and toughness, Macmillan managed to rescue his party from the consequences of Suez, while simultaneously educating it to accept the lesson. Keeping domestic policy on a moderate 'Butskellite' line, he avoided antagonising the trade unions even at the cost of sacrificing his Chancellor of the Exchequer (Peter Thorneycroft); and he was able to let the country's increasing prosperity win approval for his government.

In the face of these adverse political circumstances, the Labour Party did its best to prepare for the next election. Unquestionably, it had learnt many of the lessons of its 1955 defeat. Internal dissension was muted, for Bevan supported the majority of the party on the issue of retention of the H-bomb, saying that Britain must not go 'naked into the conference chamber'.[4] The participation of both Bevan and Wilson in the 'shadow cabinet' deprived the rebellious minority of the party of its leadership, and the organisation that existed, known as the 'Victory for Socialism' group, had little influence. The party electoral organisation gradually improved: more agents were appointed and special attention was devoted to marginal constituencies. A new policy was carefully worked out: it concentrated on the need for economic expansion and growth with government encouragement, and maintained that this expansion would provide adequate funds for an expansion of social services. It advocated an elaborate scheme for improved pensions, and a more effective educational system involving the further encouragement of Comprehensive Schools. No industries were now scheduled for nationalisation except those that the Conservatives had denationalised — steel and road haulage; but the party reserved the right to make extensions of public ownership or control when necessary.

In the course of 1959 Macmillan gained popularity for his work in improving East-West relations and paving the way for a summit meeting. A considerable consumption boom also redounded to the credit of the government, and a long-term political advertising campaign both by the Conservative Party and by other bodies including the Iron and Steel Federation encouraged the formation of a favourable 'image' of the party in the country as a whole. When the dissolution of Parliament was announced in September 1959, towards the end of one of the finest summers in recent history, the result of the forthcoming election seemed to be already assured.

Yet the Labour Party could still stage a powerful and effective campaign. Gaitskell himself made a successful tour of the country, impressing many electors with his vigour and air of sincerity. The party's television broadcasts were better than those of the Conservatives, in an election in which television counted for more than ever before. Also, the headquarter press conferences run by the party secretary, Morgan Phillips, were unexpectedly successful and won much publicity in the newspapers. Halfway through the campaign it seemed as if Labour was drawing equal with the Conservatives. At this stage, however, Labour spokesmen published various pledges not to increase taxation, and these could be construed as bribes to the electorate : it was easy for their opponents to take advantage of this. The campaign ended with opinion apparently swinging back in the Conservative favour.

The results gave the Conservative Party a considerably increased majority — a unique success for a party that had been in office already for eight years. The new House contained 365 Conservatives, 258 Labour, and 6 Liberal members, together with one Independent. The Labour share of the poll had dropped from 46·4 to 43·8 per cent; and the Liberals had more than doubled their share, partly through running more candidates and partly by increasing their vote in many of the contests. Only in Scotland and in Lancashire and Cheshire, where there was some industrial unemployment, did the Labour Party improve its position compared with 1955.

(5)

To lose three consecutive elections, by an increasing margin on each occasion — this was the fate of the Labour Party in the 1950's. It was natural that the failure of 1959 should be followed by a much more searching phase of self-examination than the party had ever undertaken before. Was the Labour Party, with its 'class' basis and its close ties with the unions, obsolete in the new Britain? Was the Liberal revival indicative of a need for a new alignment on the Left? Gaitskell himself, speaking at the brief conference of the party held a few weeks after the election, narrowed the issue to the demand for a revision of the party's objects, as laid down in the constitution. He urged the abandonment of the existing Clause Four, with its demand for 'the common ownership of the means of pro-

Hugh Gaitskell (1906-1963) and Aneurin Bevan (1897-1960)

James Callaghan (b. 1912) and Harold Wilson (b. 1916)

duction, distribution, and exchange'. After a sharp controversy within the party, however, he was forced to accept
a compromise whereby the National Executive was committed to recommending the retention of the existing clause
and the addition of a new statement of principles.

But soon the disagreements over the revision of the
constitution were swallowed up in a larger controversy over
the party's defence policy. The Campaign for Nuclear
Disarmament, which advocated the unilateral renuncia-
tion of atomic weapons, had been winning many recruits
within the party, particularly among the younger generation; and when Gaitskell in consultation with both party
and T.U.C. leaders drew up a new statement of defence
policy in the summer of 1960, he found himself faced by
strong opposition from the Left wing — not only the Nuclear
Disarmers but also a variety of opponents ranging from
out-and-out pacifists and Communist sympathisers to a
more opportunistic group who — after Gaitskell's opposition to Clause Four — wished primarily to change the party
leadership. What gave this new alliance particular strength
was its success in marshalling the union block vote, for in
addition to the usual Left minority among the unions,
Frank Cousins swung the Transport Workers against the
current defence policy. The struggle reached a climax at
the T.U.C. meeting in September and at the Labour Party
Conference in October. At the T.U.C. the official defence
policy statement was approved, but so was a conflicting
resolution from the Transport Workers — a Gilbertian
situation resulting from the compromise efforts of the
Engineers' leader, W. J. Carron. At the ensuing Labour
Party Conference, held at Scarborough, Gaitskell, deprived
of the support both of Bevan (who had recently died) and
of Morgan Phillips (who was seriously ill), fought fiercely
for the defence policy statement. After a dramatic debate
in which he and his ablest colleagues evidently won most
of the uncommitted votes of the divisional party delegates,
the statement was narrowly defeated and a resolution favour-
ing unilateral disarmament was even more narrowly carried

by a union block vote which had been determined before the debate.

A situation entirely unprecedented in the party's history had now arisen. Not only had the policy of the parliamentary leader been defeated by conference on a major issue; the vote had also caused a rift between the conference majority and the majority of the parliamentary party, who still remained committed to nuclear defence. Supported as he was by the ablest remaining parliamentary spokesmen and by the bulk of the constituency parties, Gaitskell announced that he would 'fight and fight and fight again' to secure the reversal of the decision. It remained to be seen whether he could for long remain as leader of the parliamentary party when defying a major conference decision, however narrowly carried : certainly such a situation offended against the radical traditions of the party and threatened many difficulties and embarrassments for the future. At the opening of the new parliamentary session in November he was re-elected by 166 votes as against 81 for Harold Wilson, who advocated a policy of compromise with the conference majority. Gaitskell's supporter George Brown was elected Deputy Leader in succession to Bevan. Meanwhile, partisans of both sides indulged in mutual recriminations.

Thus the last months of 1960 saw the Labour Party in a weaker state than at any time for a generation : its leadership in dispute, its policy equally indeterminate on major issues, its constitution under heavy strain, and its prestige humbled. The Liberal Party challenge, although not yet able to make any impact on the parliamentary situation, was looming on the horizon. It seemed as if the decline of the Labour Party could no longer continue. The alternatives were, complete disaster—or recovery.

Dissension and Decline (1950–60)

NOTES

1. *The Times*, 24 Oct. 1952.
2. Morrison, *Autobiography*, p. 295.
3. *Labour Party Annual Report* (1955), p. 69.
4. *Labour Party Annual Report* (1957), p. 181.

FURTHER READING

Three of the principal leaders of the party in the 1950s now have major biographies: John Campbell, *Nye Bevan*, Philip Williams, *Hugh Gaitskell* (1979) and B. Donoughue and G. W. Jones, *Herbert Morrison* (1973). See also Janet Morgan (ed.), *The Backbench Diaries of Richard Crossman* (1981) and Mark Jenkins, *Bevanism: Labour's High Tide* (1979).

For a journalistic but well-informed account of the controversies within the Labour ranks, see Leslie Hunter, *Road to Brighton Pier* (1959). S. Haseler, *The Gaitskellites* (1969), examines the views of the right-wing leadership sympathetically and in detail. For left-wing attitudes to questions of foreign policy in the first post-war decade, see Leon D. Epstein, *Britain: Uneasy Ally* (Chicago, 1954).

Different views of the party's power-structure and the role of the party conference are put by Robert T. McKenzie in his *British Political Parties* and by Saul Rose, 'Policy Discussion in Opposition', *Political Studies*, iv (1956), 126–38. See also Robert T. McKenzie, 'Policy Decisions in Opposition: A Rejoinder', *Political Studies*, v (1957), 176–82. Mr McKenzie's book, though of great value, deals inadequately with the historical role of the trade-union leadership within the party. For an account of how the succession to Attlee was determined, see the articles by Lord Williamson and Sam Watson in W. T. Rodgers (ed.), *Hugh Gaitskell, 1906–63* (1964).

Martin Harrison's *Trade Unions and the Labour Party since 1945* is also important for this period, as are the Nuffield election studies for 1951, 1955, and 1959, all of them partially or wholly prepared by David Butler.

For a study of the Campaign for Nuclear Disarmament see Richard Taylor, *Against the Bomb* (Oxford, 1988). A. J. R. Groom deals more broadly with the question in *British Thinking about Nuclear Weapons* (1974). Peggy Duff's *Left, Left, Left* (1971) is the often revealing autobiography of a *Tribune* activist.

CHAPTER VIII

The Road Back to Power
(1960–66)

(1)

THE convalescence of the Labour Party after its malaise in 1960 was surprisingly rapid. The recovery of the invalid was due, in part, to Gaitskell's success in consolidating his position within the party in 1961 and 1962 ; in part, to the emergence of new issues in national politics ; and in part, to the failure of the Conservative government to deal effectively with these issues, some of which it had itself raised.

There was a certain irony in the fact that the principal beneficiary of Gaitskell's successful fight against the Left wing was Harold Wilson, who was elected as his successor as leader in 1963. But Wilson to some extent owed his authority within the party to the fact that he had long showed sympathy with the Left, who were for the most part the natural rebels. It took some time for his erstwhile friends in the rank and file to realise that he had not only inherited the mantle of Gaitskell but also the party leader's customary tenderness towards moderate opinion in the electorate. By the time the 1964 election took place, Wilson's supremacy was recognised by all, and Labour provided the impression of a party at least as united as its opponents.

Labour's return to power in October 1964, albeit with a tiny majority, as usual strengthened the position of its leader. In the seventeen months that followed before a fresh appeal to the electorate, there was little temptation to attack a Prime Minister who had such a narrow margin of support over the opposing parties in Parliament. This did not mean that there were not serious misgivings about some of the policies being pursued, both at home and abroad. But there was every reason to make allowances for a government which was bound to ask for an early renewal of its mandate, which was dependent upon foreign bankers for its chance to restore economic solvency, and which had to take into account the waywardness of every single one of its most right-wing backbenchers in the Commons.

The election of March 1966 gave the Wilson government a good deal more than the ample parliamentary majority that it required for a normal term of office. The electoral success again increased the authority of the Prime Minister, for it was obvious that it was his personal qualities, as compared with those of Edward Heath, the new Conservative leader, that had favourably impressed the electorate since the preceding election. But undoubtedly Labour M.P.s would henceforth be freer to criticise and even to refuse to support their own government in the lobbies, conscious that this would not be likely to precipitate a change of government. On foreign policy, where there was the greatest variety of opinion, and in particular on the question of joining the Common Market, divisions were almost inevitable. But the Labour Party of the 1966 Parliament, which was freer than any of its predecessors from the trammels of a dogmatic legislative programme, or from the unspoken commitments involved in representation of the old trade-union pressure group, might well find its greatest opportunities in domestic policy, where a combination of ministerial ability and back-bench freshness might render the old divisions of Left and Right entirely out of date.

(2)

In the autumn of 1960 Gaitskell determined to secure as soon as possible a reversal of the Scarborough conference decision in favour of unilateral nuclear disarmament. In the course of the following winter and spring he campaigned up and down the country, patiently putting his case to audiences that were often hostile and sometimes disorderly. His task of winning support was much facilitated by the fact that there were still anti-unilateralist majorities not only on the executive of the parliamentary party but also on the party's National Executive (the majority of whom were union nominees) and on the General Council of the T.U.C. Representatives of these three bodies met to draw up a new defence policy statement, which, under the title of *Policy for Peace*, was submitted to the Labour Party's affiliated unions and constituency parties for consideration early in 1961.

Meanwhile Gaitskell's supporters in the unions and in the local parties had begun, for the first time, to take concerted action to rally their respective organisations to his side. A body called the Campaign for Democratic Socialism was formed, and although, unlike the Campaign for Nuclear Disarmament, it did not go in for mass demonstrations, it did co-ordinate the activities of many key party workers and union leaders who wanted to see the Scarborough decision reversed. In reality, the unilateralists had all along been a minority within the party: so the C.D.S. was virtually pushing at an open door. Its success was immediate. By the summer, three important unions — the Shop, Distributive and Allied Workers, the Engineers, and the Railwaymen — had all decided to reverse their attitude; and at the party conference at Blackpool in October the leadership's policy was endorsed by a majority of almost three to one. It was noteworthy that among the constituency parties, whose voting showed a majority for Gaitskell both at Scarborough and at Blackpool, the leadership's position had markedly improved with those parties whose local M.P.s were supporters of Gaitskell.

Gaitskell's victory was essential for the restoration of the party's prestige with the wider public. But there were other factors in the political situation which enabled this restoration to take place in short order. In July 1961 Selwyn Lloyd, the Chancellor of the Exchequer, having become worried about the competitive position of British exports, announced a 'pay pause'. This meant a recommendation to employers to hold up any pending wage increases, and at the same time a firm decision to set the example to private industry by freezing the wages and salaries of civil servants and other government employees. The 'pay pause' was highly unpopular, especially as many of those whose remuneration was financed from the Treasury, such as teachers and civil servants, already felt a sense of grievance as a result of increases in the cost of living and the advance of wage levels in private industry. At about the same time, the government made the important decision to start negotiations for the entry of Britain into the European Common Market. This decision, which threatened not merely to upset the existing Commonwealth preference system but also to involve the country in some sort of federal union of Europe, was bound to arouse intense controversy, not least within the ranks of the Conservative Party itself.

The effect of these events was soon to be seen in the national opinion polls and, even more dramatically, at by-elections. Already in the later months of 1961 the Conservatives had apparently lost their decisive measure of support in the country, and in March 1962 the Liberal challenge took its most tangible form when Orpington, formerly a safe Conservative seat, changed its allegiance and elected a Liberal. A few months later the Prime Minister, Harold Macmillan, made drastic Cabinet changes, retiring several of his senior ministers including Selwyn Lloyd and bringing younger men into key posts. Although in the long run these changes were likely to be beneficial, at the time they could not but seem to be evidence of the government's weakness.

Meanwhile a good deal of opposition to the idea of the Common Market was developing within the Labour Party, and this was particularly vocal on the Left. Rather to the surprise of some of his strongest supporters, Gaitskell shared this reaction. At the 1962 party conference at Brighton he received a tremendous ovation for a speech in which he appealed for the maintenance of the multi-racial Commonwealth and spoke of entry into the Common Market as 'the end of a thousand years of history'. When Frank Cousins indicated his union's willingness to finance the printing of a million or more copies of the speech, it seemed as if the wounds caused by the divisions within the party in the previous decade were at last beginning to heal. The recovery had been aided by the growing divergence between the government's defence policy and that of the Labour Party leadership, which brought the latter somewhat closer to the minimum aims of the nuclear disarmers. This was because of the increasing technical problems involved in providing a delivery system for nuclear weapons, which led the government into the paradoxical situation of having to purchase American missiles to use with its 'independent deterrent'. Meanwhile the Campaign for Nuclear Disarmament was disintegrating because of internal disagreements about the tactics of its most militant section, the 'Committee of 100'.

But the increasing support for the Labour Party in the country probably drew most of its strength from the economic difficulties of the time. In the winter of 1962–3 there was more unemployment than for many years, and certain regions such as Ulster and North-Eastern England were particularly hard hit. Selwyn Lloyd's restrictive fiscal policy in earlier months was regarded as being responsible for this. In addition, the winter was an exceptionally hard one, and this made unemployment still worse. There was also hardship caused by power cuts, and the government was blamed for the lack of sufficient reserve electricity plant. The main initiative that the government was undertaking in economic affairs was its attempt to join the Common Market; and this finally foundered when de Gaulle pronounced his veto in January 1963.

It was just at this moment that Hugh Gaitskell died suddenly of a rare infection. At 56, he was at the height of his powers and prestige. The long struggle that he had fought and won within the party had enhanced his public standing, and many saw him as an almost certain future

The Road Back to Power (1960–66)

Prime Minister. It was at first difficult to see who could replace him, for among those who were his closest supporters there was no one who seemed to have quite the necessary ability and stature. George Brown, the deputy leader, although possessed of many fine qualities, was felt to be too volatile a personality for the highest office. The ablest front-bench spokesman of the party, Harold Wilson, was a man of the Left. Wilson, the 'infant prodigy' of Attlee's Cabinet, was now a trenchant and witty debater as well as an expert on economic affairs. A man of humble origin who had made his way to the top by scholarships and by sheer administrative ability, he seemed in some ways to be typical of a new and important element in British society. The question for the parliamentary party was, would the quarrels of the past or the opportunities of the future determine its choice of leader? This time there was probably no strong guidance from the trade-union wing of the party. George Woodcock, the new T.U.C. secretary, had no wish for strong links with the party; and the secretaries of the larger unions were divided in their views. In the upshot, Wilson secured a decisive victory over his two opponents in the ballot, George Brown and another Gaitskellite, James Callaghan. The voting in the first ballot was: Wilson, 115; Brown, 88; Callaghan, 41. In the second ballot, Wilson was elected with 144 votes to Brown's 103.

If the wider public had any qualms about the choice, there was no evidence of it in the by-election results and the opinion polls. Wilson took care to emphasise the continuity of party policy in spite of the change of leadership. The outlines of the programme for the forthcoming election had already been laid down in the statement, *Signposts for the Sixties*, which had been endorsed by the Blackpool conference. The steel industry was to be re-nationalised, and a Land Commission was to be set up to purchase building land, but apart from this the proposals of the programme concentrated on the stimulation of economic growth by fiscal and administrative measures. At the 1963 conference — which was held, as if to exorcise the ghost of 1960, at

Scarborough — Wilson made a speech devoted to the importance of science and higher education in the new technological age. His speech made a considerable impression outside the party as well as within it.

In the course of the summer and autumn of 1963, the government's difficulties continued. In June, the Secretary for War, John Profumo, had to resign after attempting to conceal his involvement in a sordid scandal. The affair, together with other cases of rather less dramatic impact, raised serious doubts about the effectiveness of the security system against espionage, which was regarded as the Prime Minister's personal responsibility. In October Harold Macmillan, weakened by an operation, was forced to resign the Premiership, and a long-drawn-out struggle took place within the Conservative Party to choose his successor. To the press and public, R. A. Butler seemed the obvious choice, but in the end Lord Home, the Foreign Secretary, 'emerged' as the new Prime Minister. He was thought by many to know little of economic affairs, and to be out of sympathy with the younger and more progressive elements in the Cabinet. This impression was increased by the refusal of Iain Macleod to join the new government, and his sharp attack on his former colleagues.

The ensuing months of Conservative government, however, saw a certain recovery. Sir Alec Douglas-Home (as Lord Home became after renouncing his peerage) held his own quite effectively in the Commons and on television; and as fuller employment returned and, with it, a boom in consumer goods, the opinion polls pointed to the possibility of a Conservative victory at an election in the autumn of 1964. Even the weather seemed to be on the Conservative side, for a mild winter in 1963–64 was followed by the best summer of recent years. The only disturbing feature was a failure of exports to reach their expected targets, and this, taken with an adverse trend in the terms of trade, made for a marked increase in the gap between exports and imports.

When the election at last took place in October — just at the end of the permitted term of Parliament — the parties were in a position to fight on very equal terms. The Labour Party could take advantage of the government's past failings and the prospect of a repetition of the Selwyn Lloyd policy of restriction on expansion. The Conservatives could point to full employment and to the existing high standard of living, and imply that Labour policies would ruin this. Both parties did their best to ignore the Liberal challenge, which was expressed in a considerable increase in that party's list of candidates. The issue of the 'independent deterrent', which Labour proposed to abandon, made little impact in the campaign.

The result of the election all too closely reflected the two main parties' equal balance of advantage. The Labour Party, with a net gain of fifty-six seats, found itself with an overall majority in the new Parliament of only four seats. The figures were: Labour 317; Conservatives 304 (including the Speaker); Liberals, 9. This was a closer result even than in 1950. Yet while the electorate had spoken in an equivocal fashion, there was little doubt about the personal achievement of Wilson in the campaign. He had, indeed, focussed attention upon himself, by personally conducting the party's daily press conferences; and he emerged from the election with a remarkable success in his own constituency and with the knowledge that the country regarded him as potentially a better Prime Minister than his predecessor.

(3)

As soon as the election was over, Wilson lost no time in forming a government. George Brown became Deputy Premier and Minister for Economic Affairs — a new department, separated from the Treasury, and responsible for the planned growth of the economy. The other major appointments were James Callaghan as Chancellor of the Exchequer, Patrick Gordon Walker as Foreign Secretary and Denis Healey as Secretary for Defence. There were two Cabinet appointments from outside the ranks of the ordinary party leadership: Frank Cousins, the Transport Workers' secretary,

took the new post of Minister of Technology; and Lord
Gardiner, a distinguished barrister and law reformer, became Lord Chancellor. Besides Cousins, two members of
the Left wing to enter the Cabinet were Anthony Greenwood as Colonial Secretary and Mrs Barbara Castle as
Minister of Overseas Development — another new office.
The Cabinet was a large one, having twenty-three members,
and nearly all its members were older than the Prime
Minister, who at 48 was younger than any of his predecessors since Rosebery.

The omens for the success of the new government were
not favourable. The difficulties of passing legislation without an adequate working majority in the House of Commons
could be recalled all too clearly from 1950–1. The Labour
Party as a whole had hardly secured endorsement from the
electors: its victory was not due to any increase in the
number of Labour supporters, which was even lower than
in 1959. The electors had tired of Conservatism, but instead of turning to Labour, they had either abstained or
voted Liberal. The influence of the Liberal Party, whose
candidates had come second in 54 constituencies, had yet
to be determined. Finally, the new ministers found that
their predictions of an incipient economic crisis were all too
true. An unfavourable balance of trade for the year of no
less than eight hundred million pounds was expected; and
unless immediate action was taken, a disastrous flight from
the pound appeared inevitable.

The Labour leaders, and not least the Prime Minister,
seemed technically better equipped to deal with economic
problems than their predecessors of a generation earlier had
been. They at once made up their minds to resist devaluation, and to safeguard sterling they imposed a substantial
import surcharge — a temporary measure which was much
disliked abroad — and they also arranged for large credits
from foreign banks. By this means the immediate crisis was
surmounted; and in the midst of its repercussions, including
an increase in bank rate to 7 per cent, the government
settled down to work out long-term measures for putting

the trade balance right. The Department of Economic Affairs was to prepare a plan for economic growth and to secure the agreement of both sides of industry for a prices and incomes policy. The Ministry of Technology was to encourage the application of new methods in industry and to ensure the development of key manufactures such as machine tools and computers. And the Treasury was to limit the growth of public spending, including that of the nationalised industries.

Concern with the economic crisis may have prevented ministers from paying sufficient attention in the early days of the new government to their relations with the public. To begin with, these were far from happy. A projected increase in old age pensions and sickness and unemployment benefits, which was the fulfilment of an election pledge, was postponed until after Christmas on grounds of administrative difficulty; but a substantial rise in M.P.s' salaries was put into effect immediately. The result was that Gordon Walker, the Foreign Secretary, who had lost his seat at Smethwick in the General Election and who now sought re-election for the supposedly safe Labour seat of Leyton, was ignominiously defeated at a by-election in January. He was forced to resign office, being replaced by Michael Stewart; and the effective parliamentary majority of the government fell from five to three — which meant that any accident of fate could place its day-to-day control of parliamentary business in jeopardy.

To their credit, Wilson and his colleagues showed no signs of hesitation in the face of these dangers, but pushed ahead with the urgent policy decisions that were needed. A review of defence planning was initiated, and in the meantime several expensive projects for new British aircraft were abandoned, in spite of protests from both firms and workmen employed in their manufacture. George Brown in December secured the support of both employers and unions for a 'Statement of Intent' in favour of a prices and incomes policy, and in April a National Board for Prices and Incomes was set up, to consider and report upon such price increases or wage demands as were referred to it. It had no statutory powers, but it was later announced that legislation would be introduced to enforce advance notification of proposed price increases and wage claims. Callaghan's Spring Budget introduced a Capital Gains Tax and a Corporation Tax, and in spite of the narrowness of the parliamentary majority a highly complicated Finance Bill was gradually taken through all its stages. A Steel Nationalisation Bill was not attempted, but a White Paper setting out the government's proposals for a take-over was formally approved in May. To the embarrassment of the government, two of its right-wing parliamentary supporters, Woodrow Wyatt and Desmond Donnelly, expressed hostility to the measure.

Although Labour M.P.s virtually always felt obliged to support their government in the lobbies, there was a good deal of disquiet about certain of its policies, and (apart from steel nationalisation) this was as usual especially marked on the Left wing. Three major areas of controversy can be defined. One was the question of immigration by coloured people from the Commonwealth, which had greatly increased in the early 1960's. Before and during the election the party's spokesmen had criticised the Conservatives for introducing restrictions on immigration from the Commonwealth, but in areas of heavy immigration, such as the Midlands, it was clear from the election results that voters had deserted the party or abstained as a result. Indeed, Gordon Walker's initial loss of his seat at Smethwick was largely attributed to this issue. It did not take the new government very long to decide to restrict immigration even more than before. It is true that this was accompanied by proposals to prevent discrimination against immigrants already in the country. Nevertheless, there was bound to be a vigorous protest from within the party about the abandonment of the principle for which it had previously contended.

There were also the usual conflicts over foreign policy. The major issue in this period was provided by the American involvement in the war in Vietnam. The government of

South Vietnam was struggling somewhat ineffectively against Communist guerrillas, who were aided by the government of North Vietnam. American intervention on the side of South Vietnam was increasing in scale, and American bombers undertook heavy raids on targets in both South and North Vietnam, and approached the borders of China. Members of the Labour Party, and not just the Left wing, were disturbed by the diplomatic support which the government gave to the Americans. But Michael Stewart vigorously defended the policy of his department and pointed to the refusal of the North Vietnamese government to take part in any negotiations.

Finally, George Brown's incomes policy, and in particular the proposals to enforce advance notification of wage claims, worried the trade-union leaders, and an important minority led by the Transport Workers registered their opposition. The Transport Workers, now that Frank Cousins was in the Cabinet, were being led by Harry Nicholas, another left-winger who was Assistant General Secretary. But Cousins himself was thought to be in sympathy with his union's attitude, although it conflicted with George Brown's policy, to which as a Cabinet minister he was naturally committed.

All these questions were warmly debated at the party conference in September 1965, and card votes were taken on them. Fortunately for the government, the very precariousness of its parliamentary position guaranteed a friendly reception for ministers, and in any case many of the well-known spokesmen of the Left wing, particularly Cousins himself, Greenwood, and Mrs Castle, were silenced by their membership of the Cabinet. On all issues, the majorities for the official standpoint were substantial.

In the following autumn, attention was diverted from these matters by the Rhodesian government's insistence upon unconditional independence from Britain — independence, that is, for the white minority, without any safeguards for the gradual assumption of power by the black African majority. Negotiations for constitutional progress had been undertaken, but no formula acceptable to both sides could be found, and although Wilson visited Salisbury, the capital of Rhodesia, in a final attempt to break the deadlock, in November a Proclamation of Independence was made by Ian Smith, the Rhodesian Premier. While disavowing the use of military force to restore its control, the British government introduced economic sanctions to bring the now illegal Rhodesian regime to heel, but these could only be expected to prove effective — if at all — after several months. Meanwhile at the United Nations and through other channels the government acted to secure international co-operation for its methods of dealing with the situation.

Difficult though the Rhodesian problem was, in these early stages it was responsible for a revival of confidence in the Labour government. Wilson's policy did not differ markedly from that already initiated by earlier Conservative governments, and he had the reluctant support of the Conservative 'Shadow Cabinet'. There was, however, a vocal minority in the Conservative Party, led by Lord Salisbury, which sympathised with Ian Smith and opposed all sanctions. Sir Alec Douglas-Home had lately retired from the Conservative leadership; his successor, Edward Heath, had difficulty in asserting his authority at a time when the party was so divided over policy.

It was therefore by default of opposition as much as by its own merits that the government won popularity at the end of 1965. Callaghan's financial policy also helped: he appeared to take a good deal of the inflationary pressure out of the economy without causing unemployment. At the turn of the year the opinion polls were showing a substantial Labour lead, and talk of an early election was revived. In January a by-election at Hull registered a substantial increase in the Labour proportion of the poll. So at the beginning of March Wilson dissolved Parliament, claiming not unreasonably that the country needed a government with an adequate majority.

The election campaign was, on the whole, a dull one. No new policies of importance were offered to the electorate, although several of the old ones had been abandoned or considerably modified. Wilson himself presented the image of decisive but moderate leadership—in his own word 'pragmatic'. The Labour slogan for the campaign was 'You know Labour Government works'. The intellectual Socialists did not like this approach. The *New Statesman* complained that the campaign was 'a dreary wasteland where reason is excluded and the voter is presented with a purely tribal option : Heath or Wilson?' Nevertheless the results appeared to justify Wilson's methods. There was a national swing of 2·7 per cent in Labour's favour. A total of 363 Labour M.P.s were elected, as against 253 Conservatives, 12 Liberals, and one Irish Republican. Leaving aside the Speaker—who was now Dr Horace King, the first Labour M.P. to hold the office—there was an overall Labour majority of 96. The Labour Party won 47.9 per cent of the total poll, but the proportion of the electorate who actually voted was again smaller than before. Although the Liberals had gained seats, their performance in general was disappointing. The honours of the election were entirely with Labour, which for the second time in its political life was assured of a period of government with real power.

FURTHER READING

For interesting information on the way in which Gaitskell recovered control of the party in 1960–1, see K. Hindell and P. Williams, 'Scarborough and Blackpool', *Political Quarterly*, xxxiii (1962) ; L. D. Epstein, 'Who Makes Party Policy?: British Labour 1960–61', *Midwest Journal of Political Science*, vi (1962) ; and Lord Windlesham, *Communication and Political Power* (1966). D. E. Butler and Anthony King, *The British General Election of 1964* (1965), contains useful chapters on social and political change in the early 1960's. The same authors' *The British General Election of 1966* (1966) contains an account of the short Parliament of 1964–6 as well as the usual thorough study of the election. W. D. Muller, *The Kept Men?* (Hassocks, 1977) is interesting on the relationship of sponsored M.P.s with their unions.

For Harold Wilson, see Dudley Smith, *Harold Wilson* (1964), and Leslie Smith, *Harold Wilson: The Authentic Portrait* (1964). The latter, though uncritical, is more accurate on points of detail. The Prime Minister's own record of the 1964 Labour Government will be found in Harold Wilson, *The Labour Government, 1964–1970: A Personal Record* (1971). See also George Brown's more succinct and selective memoir, *In My Way* (1971). P. Foot, *The Politics of Harold Wilson* (1968) is polemical but well documented. Also of great interest is R. H. S. Crossman, *Diaries of a Cabinet Minister*, i (1975).

Lewis Minkin's detailed study, *The Labour Party Conference* (1978) refers more to this period than to any other. On relations with the Common Market, see L. J. Robins, *The Reluctant Party: Labour and the E.E.C., 1961–1975* (Ormskirk, 1979).

CHAPTER IX

Wilson and the Vicissitudes of Economic Insolvency (1966-70)

(1)

THE general election of 1966 had given the Wilson government a good deal more than the ample parliamentary majority that it required for a normal term of office. It also increased the authority of the Prime Minister, for it seemed that it was his personal qualities, as compared with those of the new Conservative leader, Edward Heath, that had won for the government its vote of confidence. The old suspicion of leadership in the party, which was a legacy of 1931, was now fading away as the parliamentary party changed in composition. The trade-union element was weaker than before: only six of the 65 new M.P.s were of the traditional trade-union type, and over half of the Labour M.P.s were now university graduates. While some people might regret the changes, nobody could deny that there was plenty of talent on the government benches.

But in spite of these advantages, it did not take more than a few months for the Prime Minister and the government to lose all the favour in public opinion that it had won in the preceding eighteen months — and more. By early 1967 the Conservatives had pulled into the lead in the opinion polls, and in 1968 they built up so formidable an advantage that it seemed impossible for Labour to recover at any future general election. There grew up an expectation in the City that Wilson's government might break up in the same way as MacDonald's had done, and that a coalition might be formed. There were indeed serious divisions inside the Cabinet, and in 1968 and 1969 there were feelings of despair among the party's most loyal supporters, both in the branches and in the trade unions. By-election swings against Labour reached the figure of 20 per cent in 1968, and there were heavy losses of seats in county and borough elections, so that Labour's control of local government was reduced to a shadow of what it once had been. In London, not only the new Greater London Council but even its inner districts, which as the London County Council had been under the control of Labour since 1934, were lost in 1967. Only in 1969–70 was there a gradual recovery of some of the lost ground. By April and May of 1970 Labour had a slight lead in the opinion polls, and Wilson decided to seek a renewal of his mandate on the strength of this and of a better showing in the local elections of the spring. But the recovery was by no means a stable one; the voluntary workers available for the campaign were fewer than in earlier elections; and the result was defeat by a margin of over forty seats. All the same, not a few Labour M.P.s who survived the defeat thought that the recovery had been remarkable; they had not expected to be able to sit in another Parliament as things were going in 1967–9.

(2)

The main reason for the government's unpopularity during most of its term lay in the failure of its economic policies. Wilson and his Chancellor, James Callaghan, started off by continuing their fight to avoid the devaluation of the pound. At the same time they were anxious to avoid returning to the 'stop-go' of Conservative economic policy, which they had so vigorously criticised in the past. Callaghan's 1966 budget did nothing to effect an immediate reduction in taxation; its main innovation was the Selective Employment Tax, designed to draw manpower from service employments into export industries: its disinflationary effects were likely to be postponed for several months. Meanwhile, there was increased pressure on the pound, largely because of a prolonged seamen's strike in May and June. In July the Cabinet debated devaluation: George Brown favoured it, but the Prime Minister was hostile and still carried with him the majority of ministers. There ensued instead a wages and prices freeze, a series of measures which included restrictions on foreign currency for holidays abroad, and an increase in purchase tax and duties on tobacco, wines and spirits. This was, indeed, 'stop-go' again, although there were no cuts in social service expenditure; and George Brown recognised that his attempt to plan economic growth through a Department of Economic Affairs, separate from the Treasury, had been defeated. At first he sought to withdraw altogether from the government, but he was induced to remain, and in August he exchanged offices with Michael Stewart, the Foreign Secretary.

Meanwhile the trade unions were smarting under the pressure of the wage freeze, which was to last six months and then to be followed by a further six months of 'severe restraint'. The government hoped that the unions would observe the freeze voluntarily, but in case of trouble it secured compulsory powers by a Prices and Incomes Act, hurriedly passed in August. Some of the union leaders, among them Frank Cousins, who had resigned from the Cabinet in July, resented the government's methods and so defied the terms of the Act, thus causing the implementation of the compulsory powers. At the Labour Party conference in the autumn, criticisms of the Act were voiced by trade-union delegates, but Wilson made it clear that he had no intention of giving way. 'At the end of the day,' he declared, 'the Government must take the final decisions in the interests of the nation as a whole.' His position was still sufficiently strong in 1966 to prevent a conference defeat on the issue.

In the winter of 1966–7 the July measures appeared to be restoring the strength of the pound, though at the cost of relatively high unemployment — 2–2½ per cent instead of 1–1½ per cent to which the country had become accustomed. Early in 1967 bank rate was reduced by successive stages and it looked as if the balance of payments was coming into surplus. The period of wage restraint came to an end in the summer, but the government disappointed its supporters by insisting on maintaining reserve powers to delay wage increases. The six-day war between Israel and the Arab States in June and the civil war in Nigeria both had adverse effects on the shaky British balance of payments owing to the oil and shipping surcharges which they caused. By the autumn it had become necessary to raise bank rate again, and confidence in sterling was waning. In November the decision was at last made to devalue sterling from $2·80 to the pound to $2·40. Just as the July measures of 1966 had meant the defeat of George Brown's economic policy, so the devaluation meant the failure of Callaghan's. Later in the same month he exchanged offices with Roy Jenkins, who had been making a success of his work as Home Secretary.

Devaluation was expected not only to cure the weakness of sterling, which it did for some time, but also to provide an immediate advantage to British exporters. At the same time, however, it was bound to increase the burden of British overseas expenditure and give a boost to the forces making for rapid inflation inside the country. To protect the economy against these dangers the government was obliged to cut defence spending abroad by arranging the gradual withdrawal of British troops from stations east of Suez (except for Hong Kong) and by cancelling a large order for American military aircraft. Much less palatable to the rank and file of the party were the measures to prevent rapid internal inflation. A charge was placed on National Health prescriptions, and the charge for dental treatment was increased by half. Free milk for pupils in secondary schools was terminated, and — the harshest blow of all — the raising of the school-leaving age from fifteen to sixteen was deferred from 1971 to 1973. Cuts were also made in the housing and road-building programmes. Lord Longford, the Lord Privy Seal, resigned from the government in protest against the measures. He was followed a few months later by the temperamental George Brown, but the latter's resignation

Wilson and the Vicissitudes of Economic Insolvency (1966–70)

was occasioned by a relatively minor disagreement with the Prime Minister. Michael Stewart returned to the Foreign Office, and the Department of Economic Affairs was downgraded — in 1969 it was to be abolished altogether. Roy Jenkins's first budget in March 1968 made further increases in indirect taxation. His policy as he described it was 'a stiff budget followed by two years of hard slog'.

The degree of public exasperation could be gauged a few days later when three by-elections were held. The average swing against the government amounted to no less than 18 per cent — and this meant that Dudley in Worcestershire, a safe seat with a Labour majority in 1966 of over 10,000, was now won by the Conservatives by an even larger margin. Part of the trouble among Labour's working-class supporters was due to the government's insistence on asserting control of wages. A new bill for this purpose was introduced into the Commons early in the year: there was to be a ceiling of $3\frac{1}{2}$ per cent on wage increases, and the government was to have powers to delay either price or wage increases for a twelve-month period. There were many abstentions among Labour M.P.s when the second reading of the bill was voted on in May, and the government majority fell to 35. In June Ray Gunter, an old-style trade-unionist who until April had served a long term as Minister of Labour — the 'bed of nails', he called it — resigned from the government, expressing disillusionment with the way policy was determined in a Cabinet 'overweighted with intellectuals'. And the sequence of electoral setbacks continued, with the loss of Labour control in many boroughs in May and further disastrous results in parliamentary by-elections. In Scotland and Wales much of the Labour vote moved into support of Nationalist candidates: in England there were massive abstentions. That autumn the Labour Party conference passed a resolution condemning the government's retention of legal powers over wages by a majority of five to one.

Devaluation was slow to stimulate an increase in exports, and the trade gap remained large throughout 1968. A devaluation of the French franc in November again increased the pressure on the pound. The result was that consumer expenditure once more had to be cut, this time by increases in purchase tax and by a scheme whereby importers had to deposit with the Customs for a period of six months half the cost of the goods they were importing. In his 1969 budget Roy Jenkins was unable to reduce the burden of taxation; on the contrary, he increased it still further. Selective Employment Tax and Corporation Tax both went up to new levels. It was apparent, however, that statutory control of wages could not be maintained beyond the term of the Prices and Wages Act, which was due to run out at the end of the year. Fortunately by that time the effects of devaluation were at last apparent and the balance of trade was moving into surplus.

In the meantime, feeling within the party had been much agitated by an attempt by the government to introduce legal sanctions into the permanent framework of industrial relations. In a White Paper published in January 1969 with the title of *In Place of Strife*, it was proposed that the Ministry of Labour, or Department of Employment and Productivity as it was now renamed, should have powers to impose a month-long conciliation period before a strike could take effect, and where appropriate to insist on a ballot of the membership of the union or unions concerned. These proposals went beyond the recommendations of the Donovan Report, which was the report of the government's own Royal Commission on Trade Unions. But public opinion favoured the plan, and so, it may be assumed, did Britain's foreign creditors. But the opposition of the trade-union leaders was bitter — all the more so for the fact that the most powerful men in the movement were now both left-wingers — Jack Jones, who had succeeded Cousins as Secretary of the Transport Workers, and Hugh Scanlon, who had taken Carron's place as leader of the Engineers. But the left was supported by a broad consensus of feeling in the entire movement, and all were fortified by the arguments of the industrial relations experts of the Oxford school who had helped to write the Donovan Report and who held that legal powers could not prevent strikes if the workers were determined to insist on withholding their labour. A specially-summoned Trades Union Congress turned down the government proposals by an overwhelming majority, and inside the Labour Party in Parliament the Cabinet found itself faced with a revolt which included not only most of the usual left-wing rebels but also a great many of those customarily most loyal to the party whip. When the Chief Whip, Robert Mellish, informed the Cabinet of the dangers of pushing ahead with the bill, the Prime Minister and Mrs. Castle, the Secretary for Employment and Productivity, were at last forced to give way. At a meeting with T.U.C. leaders they agreed to drop the penal clauses of the bill in return for an undertaking that the T.U.C. itself would do what it could to prevent or halt unofficial strikes.

In spite of this further defeat for its policies in the sphere of economics and industry, the government gradually recovered some semblance of popularity in the later months of 1969 and early 1970. The balance of payments surplus looked increasingly healthy, and in January 1970 the Chancellor felt able to withdraw the severe restrictions on currency for foreign travel. Although the 1970 budget conferred no benefits on the great majority of taxpayers, it did relieve some two million smaller taxpayers entirely from the necessity of paying income tax. Apparently as a result of these improvements, the government won back much of its lost ground in the opinion polls, and in April and May the local elections showed substantial gains for Labour. Before the end of May the Prime Minister had decided to dissolve Parliament and hold an election, although only a little over four years of the existing Parliament had been completed.

(3)

The economic difficulties of the government had the effect of severely restricting its opportunities to carry out a programme of social improvement. Yet its achievements were impressive in some directions, even if it often meant no more than maintaining the expansion implied by existing policies. In the election manifesto of 1966, Labour had promised to achieve a target of 500,000 new houses per annum by 1969–70. This figure was far in advance of the average of the last Conservative years, 1960–3, which was of the order of 310,000. At any rate the years 1966–9 produced an average figure of over 400,000. The proportion of council housing rose from about 42 per cent to 50 per cent of the total. A Leasehold Reform Act was passed in 1967 to allow holders of long leases to purchase the freehold of their homes. A Land Commission was set up to buy land for building and thus to prevent profiteering in land values, but it had little success. Public expenditure on education rose as a proportion of the gross national product from 4·8 per cent in 1964 to 5·9 per cent in 1968. The number of teachers in training increased by more than a third in the years 1964–7; the percentage of pupils staying at school after the age of sixteen increased similarly; and the student population grew by over 10 per cent per annum. It was decided to establish a University of the Air, later known as The Open University, to provide by means of television programmes, postal tuition and summer schools a system of university education for those who had missed the opportunity at the usual age. With Jennie Lee as minister for encouraging the arts and Denis Howell doing the same for sport, there was an increase of government expenditure in both these spheres.

There were important changes in the field of social security. The National Assistance Board was merged with the Ministry of Pensions and National Insurance to become the new Ministry of Social Security. Many increases in benefits took place, family allowances were more than doubled in money terms, and the redundancy payments introduced in 1965 helped to cushion the burden of unemployment for the rather larger numbers who had to experience it. Sociologists, including especially Professor Peter Townsend, complained that on a relative basis the gap between the poor and the better-off was no smaller in 1970 than in 1964. It

was partly to prevent this situation growing worse in the
long term that Richard Crossman, who held the newly-
created post of Minister for the Social Services, worked out
a scheme for earnings-related pensions; but this had not been
enacted before the dissolution of Parliament. National
Health expenditure rose from 4·2 per cent of the gross
national product in 1964 to 5 per cent in 1969, and expenditure on hospital building doubled; but here again reforms
of the service were still under consideration when the
government fell.

Steel nationalisation was enacted in 1967, and the British
Steel Corporation was set up in that year. This change,
which had for so long been a major issue of controversy
between the parties, took place without fuss, and appeared
to make little difference. More immediate in its impact on
the ordinary citizen was the Transport Act of 1968, prepared
by Mrs. Castle during her spell as Minister of Transport.
This established the principle of government grants for
transport authorities if uneconomic passenger services were
justified on social grounds. The same act set up a National
Freight Corporation to provide integrated road and rail
freight services. Public expenditure on roads went up
steadily and stricter safety precautions, including the well-
known 'breathalyser' test for drunken driving, were introduced. By the Docks and Harbours Act of 1966 and the
Dock Labour Scheme of 1967 the system of employment in
the docks was re-organised in order to put an end to casual
employment. In October 1969 a single minister, Anthony
Crosland, was placed in overall charge of the transport and
housing policy, with the title of Secretary for Local Government and Regional Planning. This was to have been the
prelude to the reorganisation of local and regional government along the lines recommended by the English and
Scottish Royal Commissions which reported in 1969.

Coloured immigration from Commonwealth countries
continued to be a sensitive political issue. A stringent
Commonwealth Immigrants Act was hurriedly passed in
1968 when it appeared that a number of Kenya Asians,

who still held British passports, were on the point of being driven out of their homeland by 'Africanisation'; they too were nearly all excluded from Britain. At the same time the government salved its conscience by carrying a Race Relations Act to prevent discrimination in employment or housing against coloured people already inside the country. It was ironic that the greatest civil conflict that arose inside the United Kingdom in the immediately succeeding years was due to the centuries-old struggle between Protestant and Catholic in Ulster. The Northern Ireland government was forced to call upon British troops to maintain order, but serious rioting involving many casualties and some deaths continued in spite of measures to eliminate discrimination against Catholics.

In its external relations the government continued to be embarrassed by the problems which had beset it in 1964 and 1965. The great bulk of Labour activists deplored the American involvement in Vietnam, and feeling grew stronger as the war intensified and atrocities were reported. But the government did not want to sever its ties of alliance with the United States, on which the defence of Western Europe against possible Russian aggression continued to be based. Attempts by the Prime Minister and by successive Foreign Secretaries to find some formula for a peace settlement were completely unsuccessful. On Rhodesia, the Prime Minister held meetings with Ian Smith in 1966 and in 1968 to try to negotiate a return to constitutional rule, but no agreement was reached and Rhodesia became a republic; sanctions imposed by the United Nations signally failed in their object of destroying the rebel regime. The African members of the Commonwealth were aggrieved by what they took to be the British government's feebleness in the face of this challenge to its authority. They were only partially mollified by the decision of the government to ban the sale of arms to South Africa. In the Nigerian civil war, there was heated controversy about whether the British policy of supporting the Federal government with arms and ammunition was a correct one or not: an unusual assortment of Left-wing and

Right-wing voices were raised in support of Biafra, but they fell silent when the Biafran collapse took place in 1969. In general, British influence in the 'Third World' was constantly declining owing to economic stringency: Overseas Aid was a declining element in the British budget and British troops were preparing to withdraw from the Far East and the Persian Gulf by 1971.

The further weakening of Britain's commitments outside Europe strengthened the case for joining the Common Market. Quite soon after the 1966 election the government decided to look into the possibility of making a fresh application to join, and in May 1967 it announced its intention of doing so. There was some opposition both within the Cabinet and in the parliamentary party, but nobody resigned, and the party conference of 1967 supported the government's change of policy on this issue. But it soon became clear that the French government remained unwilling to negotiate. President de Gaulle took the opportunity of Britain's devaluation to assert that the weakness of the British economy made the moment inappropriate. After the fall of de Gaulle in 1969, however, it became possible to make an early renewal of the application; but talks had not been resumed before the fall of the Labour government in 1970.

In considering the work of the government in the years 1966–70 it would be a mistake to omit the legislative achievements of its back-benchers, aided at times by a government generally friendly to reform. Many of the measures carried on a free vote in these years were matters of personal morality or conscience, and it was significant that most of them had been outlined by Roy Jenkins in a book entitled *Labour's Case*, published for the 1959 election. As Home Secretary in 1966 and 1967, Jenkins was able to help back-benchers with similar views to his own to formulate and to carry these reforms. The Sexual Offences Act, 1967, legalised homosexual acts between 'consenting adults', and the Medical Termination of Pregnancy Act of the same year (introduced by a Liberal M.P. but largely supported from the Labour benches) legalised abortion if two doctors certified that it was desirable on medical or psychological grounds. A Family Planning Act gave powers to local authorities to establish an advisory service on family planning techniques if they wished to do so. In 1968 a Theatres Act was passed with government drafting assistance: it abolished the censorship of plays by the Lord Chamberlain. A Divorce Reform Act of 1969 made divorce simpler to obtain: the criterion was now 'the irretrievable breakdown of marriage', and divorce was to be obtainable after two years of separation, if there was mutual consent, and after a five-year period if there was not. A Matrimonial Property Act was also passed to give the wife an equal share in family assets when divorce took place. Finally, in December 1969, on the initiative of Callaghan who was then Home Secretary, but on a free vote of both Houses, the abolition of the death penalty, enacted for a five-year period in 1965, was turned into a permanent measure. A total of 279 Labour M.P.s voted for this and only three against, whereas the majority of the Conservative party opposed it.

(4)

By the spring of 1970, as we have seen, the improvement in the balance of payments was beginning to incline the electorate to take a more favourable view of the Labour Government. But many traditional elements of support for Labour had been alienated, and the local parties had been seriously weakened. Trade-union officials had been offended at the attempt to impose legal restrictions on the right to strike, and were slow to rally to the party in 1970. Students and young people generally, affected by the spirit of discontent which was so prominent in the United States, France and elsewhere, gave Labour little credit for what liberal reform it enacted and what social services it expended. The chances of winning an election, therefore, seemed to depend upon gaining the approval of a large proportion of the 'floating voters' — probably a growing element — who

tended to judge governments strictly by their capacity to
deal with national problems. Wilson had, of course, bid
for their support in 1964 and 1966; but this time he was
more dependent upon them than ever.

In May the opinion polls suggested that this body of
electors was swinging back to the support of the Labour
Party. In any poll comparing the two party leaders, Wilson
always did much better than Heath; and so once again
Wilson sought to make the election a choice, for the uncommitted, between his own personality and that of the Opposition Leader. This meant that he tried to play down the
issues of principle between the parties on such matters as
nationalisation or even race relations. The emphasis was
to be on Labour's success in overcoming the adverse balance
of trade, and on the relatively uncontroversial case for
planning of the environment. The election manifesto, with
a photograph of Harold Wilson on the cover, was entitled
Now Britain's Strong Let's Make It Great to Live In. For most
of the election campaign this strategy seemed to be working
successfully, and until polling day itself (18 June) the
opinion polls pointed to a Labour victory. But to the
general surprise, the constituencies swung to the Conservatives by an average of 4·7 per cent, which was enough to
give Edward Heath a majority of 31 in the new Parliament.
Compared with 1966, the Labour Party lost 74 seats and
returned to the Commons with a total of 287 M.P.s (excluding the Speaker) as against 330 for the Conservatives. The
Liberals also lost ground and were reduced to six; and there
were six independents, mostly representing Northern Ireland.
There was a drop in the proportion of the electorate who
went to the poll, from 76 per cent in 1966 to 72 per cent in
1970. Although this was partly accounted for by the fact
that many people had gone on holiday in June, there was
probably also a certain amount of apathy due to the quiet-
ness of the campaign. For the first time the electorate
included young people aged between 18 and 21, who had
been enfranchised by an act of 1969.

Observers had great difficulty in deciding why the

opinion polls were so misleading about the election.' There
was some evidence to suggest that the publication of a bad
set of trade figures just three days before election day had
an adverse effect on Labour supporters.   There was also
a revival of controversy about Commonwealth immigration,
for which Enoch Powell, the former Conservative minister,
was responsible ; but as this issue tended to arouse concern
only in certain parts of the country, whereas the swing
against Labour was remarkably uniform, it seems unlikely
that it played much part.   More importance should probably
be attached to the efficiency of the Conservative Party
organisation, as compared with Labour's meagre resources.
It was probably a misfortune for the Labour Party that when
Len Williams retired from the post of party secretary in
1968 he was replaced, not by an efficient and relatively
young executive, as was originally intended, but by an old
hand from the Transport Workers, Harry Nicholas, who
could not be expected to make any radical changes.   But
above all, there was the sense of disillusion among so many
of the former supporters of the party.   There were wounds
that could heal only with time and by reaction to the unfriendly policies of a new Conservative government.

FURTHER READING

Clive Ponting's *Breach of Promise* (1989) is an interesting and well-
informed assessment, if perhaps somewhat unduly severe, of the record
of Labour rule in the 1960s. Harold Wilson's *The Labour Government,
1964–1970* is of course authoritative, but it is difficult to see the wood
for the trees in its 800 breathless pages. George Brown's *In My Way*
is far more readable. R. H. S. Crossman, *Diaries of a Cabinet Minister*,
ii and iii (1976 and 1977) describe in intimate detail the day-to-day
pressures of government. P. Jenkins, *The Battle of Downing Street* (1970) is
a journalist's skilful reconstruction of the conflict within the Labour
Party over *In Place of Strife*, subsequently confirmed by Crossman. For
an account of the role of the Trade Union Group of M.P.s in the struggle,
see the Fabian pamphlet by J. Ellis and R. W. Johnson, *Members from
the Unions* (1974). B. Hindess, *The Decline of Working-Class Politics*
(1971) develops an interesting thesis as suggested by its title, but the
evidence for the thesis is only localised. On the 1970 election, see D.
Butler and M. Pinto-Duschinsky, *The British General Election of 1970*
(1971).

CHAPTER X

The Common Market and the Social Contract (1970-79)

(1)

In the five years after the election defeat of June 1970, the Labour Party managed to avoid the fate that had befallen it after its earlier spell of power in the 1940s, of remaining in the wilderness for more than a decade. But it returned to office in March 1974 only as a minority government, and in the second election of October of that year it improved its position no more than marginally, so as to have an overall majority of just three seats—soon to be whittled away by lost by-elections and defections to a minority again.

Harold Wilson was the only Prime Minister in the post-war period to form a new ministry after a defeat at the polls. But the inheritance of economic misfortune which in large part accounted for his second chance was a harsh one : an unprecedented inflation rate and an economy which was exceptionally sluggish. In this situation, many electors turned away from the two main parties and voted either for the Liberals or, in Scotland and Wales, for the Nationalist Parties. In Northern Ireland, after the suspension of the Stormont Parliament in 1972, the Unionists had become completely alienated from their earlier ties with the British Conservatives. As for the Labour Party in Britain, even when it won, its proportion of the vote was little more than in 1929, when the Liberals still held the balance of power. Both its individual membership and the number of its full-time agents were far below the figures of the early 1950s. And serious tensions reappeared between the majority of the Parliamentary Party on the one hand and the National Executive and the Annual Conference on the other. The new General Secretary, Ron Hayward, assumed a more than administrative rôle and made speeches on policy which sharply diverged from government views. In the face of these difficulties Harold Wilson performed a balancing act the skill of which was more impressive to those who could appreciate the finer points of political manoeuvring than to those who could not. And he could even claim after the second election of 1974 that Labour was 'now the natural party of government'.

(2)

An election defeat, and particularly an unexpected election defeat such as that of June 1970, might well have led to some recrimination within the party ranks. That this did not take place on any large scale was a tribute to Wilson's authority and prestige, which had recovered well in the spring of that year. He was re-elected unopposed to the Leadership, and interest centred on the Deputy Leadership, for George Brown had been defeated in the election and had then accepted a peerage. Roy Jenkins, who had been a successful Chancellor of the Exchequer, and who was now the most prominent of the party's right wing, easily defeated his rivals Michael Foot and Fred Peart. The elections for the Shadow Cabinet also turned out well for the right wing and for those who supported Britain's entry into the Common Market. But the trade union leadership was predominantly left-wing, as became clear at the Party Conference in October. Wilson initiated one major reform of the machinery of the parliamentary party when he decided to cede the post of Chairman, which was usually combined with that of Leader when the party was in opposition. This freed him for the task of writing his memoirs; but it also gave him a position of independence should the Parliamentary Party and the National Executive or the Conference have a major disagreement in the ensuing months or years.

The issue that was likely to cause most conflict was that of entry into the Common Market. The new Conservative Government under Edward Heath took up the briefs which had been prepared for Labour's ministers, and went off to

Brussels and elsewhere on the Continent to negotiate. But already at the Labour Party Conference in October 1970 a resolution altogether opposing entry was very nearly carried —against the advice of the National Executive. One ex-minister, Peter Shore, had already declared his total opposition to entry before the general election ; another, Anthony Wedgwood Benn, though still in favour, declared for a referendum ; and in 1971 132 Labour M.P.s signed an Early Day Motion against the terms 'so far envisaged'. As the government's success in the negotiations became evident, the National Executive decided, by a majority of one, to hold a Special Conference in mid-July to discuss the issue : but it was agreed that this Conference was not to take any binding vote, which was to wait for the usual Annual Conference in October. At the Special Conference, the Party Chairman, Ian Mikardo, scrupulously called spokesmen from the two sides of the argument in turn, but Harold Wilson, in his closing speech, indicated clearly that the terms accepted by the government would not have satisfied him.

Eleven days later, on 28th July 1971, the National Executive voted by sixteen to six to oppose entry on the existing terms, and 'invited' the Parliamentary Party to do likewise. The minority included Roy Jenkins, the Deputy Leader, and Mrs. Shirley Williams, probably the ablest and certainly the most popular of a younger group of M.P.s. Naturally the National Executive's attitude was overwhelmingly approved both by the T.U.C. and by the rank and file of the party at the two annual conferences in September and October. There were those who pointed out that if Labour had still been in power the terms secured by the Conservatives would have been accepted both by the Cabinet and by the Parliamentary Party. But as it was, the Shadow Cabinet committed the Parliamentary Party to opposition to the principle of entry when the vote was taken on 28th October.

The right-wing members of the party who continued to support Market entry were now, for their consistency, regarded as 'rebels', and there was pressure upon them from the Parliamentary Whips and in many cases from their constituency parties to toe the new line. But, led by Roy

Jenkins and 'whipped' by William Rodgers, a former junior minister who had played an important part in the organisation of the Campaign for Democratic Socialism in 1961, they received a final piece of encouragement when the Conservatives shrewdly decided to allow a free vote to members of their own party, calculating that their own defectors would be fewer. In the end, therefore, the revolt against the Labour Whip was massive: sixty-nine M.P.s voted for Market entry on the existing terms, and twenty abstained. The vote in favour of the principle of entry was thus very convincing: it was carried by 356 to 244. It was noted shortly afterwards that 'of 23 Cabinet Ministers in the outgoing [i.e. Labour] Cabinet, only 9 voted against entry'.

When it came to the details of the enabling legislation, the Labour 'rebels' sided more often with their own party and against the government; and the Conservative 'rebels' did likewise. Partisan loyalty was encouraged by sharp clashes on other issues, for instance industrial relations, unemployment and the Housing Finance Bill. There was, however, a small group of Labour M.P.s who insisted on abstaining, and who probably thereby saved the government from defeat in the lobbies. The party's confidence in Roy Jenkins as Deputy Leader was apparently unabaited, as was shown in the annual election in November 1971, when he almost secured an outright majority on the first ballot — 140 votes, as against 96 for Michael Foot and 46 for Wedgwood Benn.

The uneasy compromise within the party leadership was however broken in April 1972, when the Shadow Cabinet decided to support a proposal by the Conservative anti-Market M.P.s that there should be a referendum before Britain's accession to the Community. This was too much for Labour's pro-Market M.P.s, and Roy Jenkins thereupon resigned the Deputy Leadership, and George Thomson and Harold Lever left the Shadow Cabinet with him. It should be noted, however, that all the other countries preparing to join the Community at the same time — Ireland, Denmark, and Norway — did hold referenda. Jenkins was replaced as Deputy Leader by Edward Short, a 'middle-of-the-road' nominee already three years older than Harold Wilson.

The European Communities Bill that the government had to carry to assure Britain's adherence to the Common Market was passed through all its stages by October 1972, and took effect from 1st January 1973. Meanwhile, there were further repercussions of the conflict within the Labour Party. Dick Taverne, the M.P. for Lincoln, was asked by his constituency party to retire, and he chose to resign his seat at once and to fight a by-election as an independent. The record of independent members in the post-war House of Commons had been very poor, and his colleagues naturally tried to dissuade him from this course. But the by-election, which the Labour Whips succeeded in postponing until March 1973, was a resounding victory for the ex-M.P. George Thomson, another pro-Market M.P. and ex-Minister, was appointed by the Heath Government as one of Britain's two Market Commissioners at Brussels. He took with him as his *chef de cabinet* Gwyn Morgan, the Party's Assistant General Secretary, who had just been defeated, by the casting vote of the chairman, Anthony Wedgwood Benn, in the National Executive's election of a successor to Harry Nicholas, the retiring General Secretary. The successful candidate for the General Secretaryship was Ron Hayward, the former National Agent, who was an opponent of entry to Europe : his election was confirmed at the 1972 Party Conference.

(3)

Meanwhile the government's legislation to deal with the unions had also been placed upon the Statute Book. The Industrial Relations Act, long nurtured within the Conservative Party by Robert Carr, who in 1970 became Secretary for Employment, was passed in 1971. Although Labour ex-ministers were in some difficulty about opposing all sections of the bill, in view of its similarity to the proposed legislation of 1969, there was bitter opposition both in Parliament and in industry, where trade unions held one-day strikes to make known their feeling. The new Act meant that unions were to register more formally than before, and a National Industrial Relations Court was set up to deal with what were now illegal practices such as unofficial strikes, sympathy strikes, the refusal of employers to recognise registered unions, and breaches of legally binding contracts. The Court could also, at the request of the Secretary for Employment, order a conciliation period before a strike began, and/or a ballot of the union membership to find out if the proposed strike had majority support. Further, the pre-entry 'closed shop' was outlawed, although a union could secure the 'agency shop' — that is to say, the sole right to represent the workers in a particular company or company shop — by agreement with the employer or by securing a majority in a secret ballot.

The unions had always been hostile to restrictive legislation, and they mostly took great exception to the creation of a special court to assist in the operation of the Act. The T.U.C. ordered its member bodies not to register under the Act, and all but a tiny minority followed these instructions. The unions also mostly refused to put their case to the National Industrial Relations Court. The conciliation delay and the secret ballot were both imposed upon the railway unions in the spring of 1972, but the result was very disappointing for the government as both devices served only to reinforce the position of the union executives. There were also two major cases brought before the Court, both involving the Engineers, who were on each occasion fined substantial sums: the union failed to pay and its assets were distrained. It responded by calling a series of one-day strikes.

The battle against the Act brought the T.U.C. and the Labour Party closer together than they had been since Attlee's day. The party became committed, as early as its 1971 Conference, to a complete repeal of the Act 'in the first session of a new Labour Government'; and the Executive was also instructed to formulate 'in consultation with the General Council of the T.U.C.' new proposals 'based upon voluntary reform'. This led in January 1972 to the formation of a powerful T.U.C.-Labour Party Liaison Committee, which decided as a first step towards better industrial relations to establish as soon as possible a non-governmental but publicly funded Conciliation and Arbitration Service.

The Common Market and the Social Contract (1970–79)

One of the main objects of the Conservative Government's Industrial Relations Act had been to reduce the incidence of strikes : but the short-term effect was precisely the reverse. The number of working days lost in 1972, at about 24 million, was the highest since 1926, the year of the General Strike. Contributing to this early in the year were the Mineworkers, who called the first national strike in their industry since 1926. Although coal stocks were high, the miners picketed the power stations to prevent any type of fuel being admitted. These tactics led to a government climb-down and to a large increase in miners' pay much as they had demanded. The result was a further twist to the inflationary spiral : but as yet the government refused to adopt a compulsory wages policy, believing that the experience of the Wilson Government showed that it would not work. Later in the year, however, the Cabinet was driven to impose a 90-day standstill on pay, prices, dividends and rents. In the spring of 1973 strict controls were introduced to monitor any further inflation, with the establishment of a Price Commission and a Pay Board. And so the Conservatives came full circle despite their election promises.

It is possible that the government's policy of curbing both wages and prices would have proved successful, had it not been for the Yom Kippur War between Egypt and Israel in the autumn of 1973. This led to a sharp increase in the price of oil charged by the Arab oil producers, designed to penalise the advanced countries of the West. In Britain, the result was more inflation and more concern about problems of energy supply. The Mineworkers put in for a large new pay claim, but this time the government refused to give way, although many people preferred to reward them rather than the Arab sheiks. The dispute began with the union merely imposing an overtime ban ; but the government felt obliged to take emergency action to limit fuel consumption, including the banning of television after 10.30 p.m., and then, from 31st December, 1973, a three-day working week for industry.

At the end of January 1974 the Mineworkers held a ballot on the proposal for a national strike. This was normal practice in their union, and not a measure imposed by the Industrial Relations Act. By an 81 per cent majority of those voting, the ballot empowered the executive to take action, and it was announced that a national strike would begin on 10th February. But at this point Edward Heath, who clearly felt that he could not afford a second defeat by the miners, decided to call a snap general election for 28th February. The issue would be the power of the unions, and not approval of Common Market entry, on which many people were probably indifferent or hostile.

The Labour Party was by now committed to a far more left-wing programme than previously in its history. But because of the issue of the election, Harold Wilson was able once more to appear as the pragmatic reconciler bent upon industrial peace, and the party manifesto was entitled *Let Us Work Together*. It promised nevertheless not only repeal of the Industrial Relations Act and renegotiation of the terms of entry to the Common Market, but also a 'fundamental and irreversible shift in the balance of power and wealth in favour of working people and their families'. This involved a wealth tax and a capital transfer tax and the nationalisation of development land and mineral rights. There was to be an extension of nationalisation also in the engineering industry and, in accordance with plans worked out by a sub-committee of the National Executive in 1972-3, a National Enterprise Board was to be set up to supervise the work of publicly owned companies. The manifesto also used the term 'Social Contract' to indicate the type of understanding which a Labour Government would hope to achieve with the trade unions, whereby the unions would co-operate in wage restraint in return for action against prices and rents and social inequality. The idea of the Social Contract emerged from the meetings of the T.U.C.-Labour Party Liaison Committee in the preceding months.

To begin with the campaign did not proceed very well for the Labour Party. Its pledges included a promise not to introduce a statutory wages policy, and Hugh Scanlon, when asked to explain how the Social Contract would work, said that he knew of no firm commitment by the unions. On the other hand, Enoch Powell, the Conservative ex-minister to whom Edward Heath had refused a place in his ministry, declared that he would vote Labour as that party favoured a referendum on the Market ; and Campbell Adamson, the Director-General of the Confederation of British Industry, the employers' pressure-group, called for the repeal of the Industrial Relations Act.

Analysis of opinion polls during the election campaign suggested that the principal features of the electorate's reaction were 'volatility' and 'depolarisation' : these were the words of a spokesman of the Harris Poll. 'Volatility' meant more voters than before changing their minds during the campaign ; 'depolarisation' meant the middle class becoming less strongly committed to the Conservatives, and the working class less committed to Labour. All this, together with the increased strength of the minor parties—the Liberals and the Scottish and Welsh Nationalists—made the election, as the *Economist* put it, 'enough to give a psephologist a nervous breakdown'. It was no doubt partly the result of the haste with which the election had been called : people reacted rather as they would have done in a by-election. Labour won the largest number of seats, 301 to the Conservatives' 297 : but they polled rather less votes by about a quarter of a million, and their proportion of the total poll, at 37·1 per cent, was lower than in any election since 1931, and in fact just equal to that of 1929. The Liberals won 19·3 per cent but were disappointed to secure only fourteen seats ; and there were 23 'Others' in the new House, including 11 Ulster Unionists, 7 Scottish Nationalists and 2 Welsh Nationalists.

After the results were known, seeing that no party had secured a majority, Heath invited Jeremy Thorpe, the Liberal leader, to Downing Street and suggested a Coalition. But Thorpe could not agree to the terms offered, and so on Monday 4th March—four days after the election—Heath resigned and Harold Wilson was again invited to form a ministry. Wilson at once announced that his government would be a genuine minority administration, and that he would make no deals with other parties. The shades of 1931 and the 'treachery' of Ramsay MacDonald still hovered over Labour in the 1970s.

(4)

In the new government Edward Short, the Deputy Leader, became Lord President of the Council and Leader of the House of Commons; James Callaghan became Foreign Secretary, and Denis Healey Chancellor of the Exchequer. Roy Jenkins, who had been re-elected to the Shadow Cabinet in November 1973, had to be content with a return to the Home Office; and the veteran left-winger Michael Foot, who had not held office before, took the post of Secretary for Employment. A new post was that of Secretary for Prices and Consumer Protection, which went to Mrs. Shirley Williams. Anthony Crosland became Secretary for the Environment (which meant Transport, Local Government and Housing); Barbara Castle took over Health and Social Security; Anthony Wedgwood Benn, now inclined to call himself simply Tony Benn, was the new Secretary for Industry; and Peter Shore was Secretary for Trade. In the new parliamentary party there was something of a shift to the Left: of the 54 new Labour M.P.s, 26 joined the Tribune Group, and Ian Mikardo, a veteran Tribune supporter, was elected Chairman of the parliamentary party.

The miners' strike was settled at once, on terms which afforded the men something of a victory, but which, it turned out, the Conservatives would have been quite willing to accept; and the three-day week was brought to an end. Subsidies were given to basic foods — bread, flour, butter, cheese, milk and tea. Michael Foot introduced bills to repeal the Industrial Relations Act and to abolish the Pay Board. For the former purpose, a new Trade Union and Labour Relations Act was passed: it was amended both in the Lords and in the Commons and did not have all the features that the government would have liked — but at least it disposed of the Conservative Industrial Relations Act. Meanwhile Denis Healey introduced two budgets, one in March and another in July. The first was generally of a standstill nature, but the second was mildly reflationary and included a cut in Value Added Tax from 10 to 8 per cent. The second budget had the effect of temporarily slowing the increase in the cost of living ; there was also a freeze on rent increases, and the Housing Finance Act of 1972 was replaced by a new Rent Act.

Disagreements within the government over the future of Britain's relations with the Common Market continued, and there was a certain amount of sniping even between Cabinet ministers on the broad principles of policy, with Tony Benn taking the lead in the call for widespread nationalisation and Roy Jenkins and Reg Prentice, the Minister for Education, arguing for 'moderation'. By the end of the parliamentary session the government had been defeated in the Commons on some twenty occasions on major policy amendments to bills : this was apart from defeats in standing committees. By September, therefore, everyone was expecting a new general election, and on the eighteenth the Prime Minister announced that it would take place on 10th October.

Being the second general election within seven months — a shorter period than any since the seventeenth century — this one could not raise the interest or enthusiasm of its predecessor. On this occasion the Labour manifesto was called *Britain will Win with Labour*. It re-emphasised the pledges of the February manifesto and laid further stress on the Social Contract with the unions, for whose benefit it promised the removal of the opposition amendments to the Trade Union and Labour Relations Act of the summer. It also promised an Employment Protection Act providing new rights for workers in industry. A new phrase in the manifesto ran as follows : 'The next Labour Government will create elected assemblies in Scotland and Wales.' On the Common Market, the government pledged itself to 'give the British people the final say' within twelve months, but declared that 'it is as yet too early to judge the likely results of the tough negotiations which are taking place'.

In the campaign the two main party leaders, Wilson and Heath, played a subdued part, and it was left to the lesser figures in the parties to make the headlines. Mrs. Margaret Thatcher, for the Conservatives, promised $9\frac{1}{2}$ per cent mortgages if her party won; and Mrs. Shirley Williams said bluntly that she would leave active politics if the Common Market ballot resulted in Britain's withdrawal. In the final stages of the campaign Heath began to speak of a 'National Coalition' government in which all parties would be invited to join. There seems to be some evidence that this struck a responsive chord in an electorate which for the most part was bored by the new contest.

In the upshot Labour secured the overall majority it had sought, but it was a tiny one — no more than three. Labour won 319 seats, as against the Conservatives' 277 and the Liberals' 13. There were now also 11 Scottish and 3 Welsh Nationalists, and the 12 Irish independents, mostly Unionists, included Enoch Powell, who returned to Parliament for South Down. There was an overall swing of 2·2 per cent from Conservative to Labour, and Transport House had the satisfaction of seeing the Liberal challenge beaten back and of recapturing the three seats occcupied by rebels from its own ranks, including that of Dick Taverne at Lincoln. But if the Labour proportion of the total poll had risen slightly — it was now 39·2 per cent — the numbers voting Labour were fewer than in February as the turnout was reduced. And they were 2½ million less than in 1951, when the party secured its highest vote ever. The only consolation for the government was to be found in the weakness of the Conservatives, who had virtually ceased to have any strength in Scotland or the North.

(5)

In the new Parliament the Labour majority was in theory exiguous but in practice adequate, as the other parties rarely co-operated in opposition. This was just as well, for the Parliamentary Labour Party was riven with faction, partly over the Common Market and partly over domestic policy. The Tribune Group was claiming to subordinate the Cabinet to the will of Conference and the National Executive, and in this they had the support of the new General Secretary, Ron Hayward.

This did not prevent Wilson and Callaghan from re-nego-
tiating the Common Market terms, slightly improving them
in Britain's favour, and in March of 1975 persuading the
Cabinet to agree to recommend a 'Yes' vote in a Referendum,
which was later fixed for 5th June. For some weeks, while
the Referendum campaign took place, ministers 'agreed to
differ', and the right and centre of the party sided with the
Conservatives and Liberals against their colleagues Michael
Foot, Barbara Castle, Tony Benn and Peter Shore, who
all put the anti-Market case. Late in April Wilson addressed
a special pre-Referendum Conference of the Labour Party
in London, which voted against his recommendation by
3,724,000 to 1,986,000 — a result which was rather more
encouraging for the pro-Market forces than had been expected, for the bulk of the 'anti' vote was made up of the
Transport Workers and the Engineers. But Wilson promised
to accept the verdict of the electorate on Referendum Day,
and the National Executive for its part recognised the right
of 'every individual to express his point of view'. The General
Secretary announced that the Executive would 'view with
disfavour any attempts at local party level to discipline
members holding minority views'. This tolerant attitude
was important in keeping the Party together at a crucial
moment.

For the battle turned out in the end to be an unequal one.
On the one side were the Prime Minister, the Cabinet
majority, and the great bulk of the Conservative and Liberal
Parties; on the other side, the Cabinet minority, many
Labour M.P.s and rank-and-file workers, and most but not
all of the big unions, together with a small minority of
Conservatives. The supporters of the 'Yes' vote were
marshalled in a body called the European Movement, which
was well financed by industry: on its platforms leaders such
as Edward Heath, Roy Jenkins and Jeremy Thorpe met in
harmony. On the other side was the National Referendum
Campaign, an ill-assorted collection of left-wing M.P.s and
trade-unionists and right-wing Tories, with very little in the
way of financial resources. In the end, the aggregate vote
for the United Kingdom resulted in a landslide victory for

the 'Yes' side : 67·2 per cent, as against 32·8. Although the results were declared county by county, there was as Wilson said a 'consistent pattern of positive voting over almost every county and region of the United Kingdom'. Only Shetland and the Western Isles of Scotland returned negative majorities. The turnout, at 64 per cent, was not unreasonably small for a much badgered electorate.

After the result the Left wing of the party in Parliament was distinctly weakened. Eric Heffer, one of the most left-wing members of the government, had already been asked to resign owing to his defiance of the Prime Minister's guidelines for the conduct of the debate, whereby opponents of the majority decision of the Cabinet were only allowed to speak against it 'in the country' and not in the House. Now Wilson made Benn exchange offices with Eric Varley, the Secretary for Energy, and removed Judith Hart from the Government. In November 1974 Ian Mikardo had failed to secure re-election as the Chairman of the parliamentary party, and in December a new group inside the party was formed called the Manifesto Group. Consisting of right and centre M.P.s, it was evidently designed as a counter-weight to the Tribune Group.

Meanwhile the Cabinet and also, very significantly, some of the leading left-wing trade unionists, were coming round to the need for an effective wages policy. Jack Jones of the Transport Workers proposed the idea of a flat-rate increase for the year 1975–6, and this was taken up by the Cabinet in a White Paper of July : the terms were to be a maximum of £6 per week increase for the entire year, with no increase at all for persons receiving over £8,500. The government sought to enforce the policy by action against employers in the private sector, by the limitation of prices, and by restricting public sector payments from the Exchequer. The policy was approved at the Trades Union Congress in September, and in the summer and autumn both the Engineers and the Miners fell into line. But in the winter of 1975–6 inflation was still in double figures ; unemployment was running at about 5 per cent ; and the government continued to be unpopular.

(6)

The whole country was taken by surprise when, late in March 1976, Harold Wilson, shortly after his sixtieth birthday, suddenly announced his intention of retiring. He had led the party for thirteen years and had been Prime Minister four times; but he seemed in good health, and his abrupt departure — not completely abrupt, for he waited for three weeks, until the parliamentary party could elect a successor — seemed puzzling. There were six candidates for the vacant post, and after two ballots it became a contest between James Callaghan and Michael Foot, the latter as so often the candidate of the Left. In the final ballot, declared on 5th April, Callaghan secured 176 votes to Foot's 137. Certainly the Left had polled far better than had been expected, and the principal right-wing candidate, Roy Jenkins, had retired after the first ballot. In Callaghan's new government Edward Short and Barbara Castle were retired, and Foot became Lord President of the Council, responsible for the devolution plans which had previously been Edward Short's concern. Anthony Crosland became Foreign Secretary, and Peter Shore succeeded him as Secretary for the Environment. There were four new Cabinet ministers, and Michael Cocks succeeded Bob Mellish as Chief Whip.

As the new financial year of 1976–7 began, the government again became a minority in Parliament, because of the defection of John Stonehouse, a former minister who was deeply in debt and who had caused a sensation by staging a disappearance in the United States and then being rediscovered in Australia. But in the course of the summer the T.U.C. agreed to a second year of wage restraint: in return for some tax relief, wage increases were to be held down to a norm of $4\frac{1}{2}$ per cent, with a minimum of £2.50 per week and a maximum of £4. In September changes took place which were consequential upon the change of leadership. Roy Jenkins left the Cabinet, having been invited by Callaghan to become Britain's senior Commissioner to the Common Market and (as a result of the rotation of offices by nationality) its President for a term beginning in January 1977. Merlyn Rees took Jenkins's place as Home Secretary;

and among other changes Shirley Williams became Secretary for Education and Roy Hattersley took her place as Secretary for Prices. In this way the strength of the party's right wing was preserved within the Cabinet.

At the same time, the Left appeared to revive its spirits after its defeat over the Referendum. It was anxious to see more nationalisation of industry in spite of the passing of the Industry Act of 1975, which had set up the National Enterprise Board—a body that took over several ailing firms including British Leyland and Ferranti. Tribunite ideas prevailed upon the National Executive and this led to sharp clashes with right-wing ministers led by Callaghan. The Party Conference in late September went on record as opposing direct elections to the European Parliament—in spite of a pledge already given by the Foreign Secretary—and in favour of the nationalisation of the clearing banks and major insurance companies. In October Michael Foot was elected Deputy Chairman of the parliamentary party by 166 votes against 128 for Mrs Williams, the right-wing contender. In the ensuing parliamentary session one further important measure of nationalisation went ahead—the Aircraft and Shipbuilding Industries Bill, which reached the statute book in March 1977.

Meanwhile British exports were still far from buoyant. Both unemployment and inflation remained high; and the early autumn of 1976 witnessed an additional and unexpected slide in the international value of sterling. Denis Healey, the Chancellor, was obliged to seek a fresh loan from the International Monetary Fund, and this time the Fund imposed strict conditions for the limitation of public spending and for the restriction of the public sector borrowing requirement. It was not quite 1931 over again : but it did call for much heart-searching among Labour supporters to accept this package at a time of high unemployment. Healey announced a further series of spending cuts, to add to those of February and July. But the parliamentary party proved restive, and 26 back-bench Labour M.P.s voted against the government motion approving the cuts. Meanwhile the party's position in the Commons had been weakening still further. In July two Scottish Labour M.P.s, after setting up a new Scottish Labour Party to hasten devolution, had resigned the Westminster whip; and in November two Labour seats were lost to the Conservatives at by-elections. But the government soldiered on with its Devolution Bill for Scotland and Wales, which had the support of both the Scottish and Welsh Nationalist Parties. Unfortunately, however, there were enough of its own supporters alienated by the Bill for the defeat of a motion in February 1977 designed to fix a timetable for its further progress. In February also the government received a severe blow in the sudden death of Anthony Crosland, the Foreign Secretary and clearly one of its ablest members. He was succeeded by Dr David Owen, his Minister of State and, at 38, the youngest Foreign Secretary for forty years.

At this point the government was in grave difficulties in view of its inability to command a Commons majority. It would have suited the Conservatives to hold an early election; and in mid-March Mrs Thatcher (who had succeeded Edward Heath as their leader in 1975) put down a motion of No Confidence. This prompted Callaghan and Foot to seek allies in other parties; and after a fruitless discussion with the Leader of the Ulster Unionist Coalition they made an agreement with David Steel, the Liberal Leader, whereby his party would support the government in return for a Labour-Liberal Consultative Committee to examine policy and proposals for legislation. The Liberals were particularly interested in the resurrection of plans for devolution and in the introduction of direct elections for the European Parliament, and the Labour spokesmen indicated that they would prepare legislation to attain these objects. The agreement led to the defeat of Mrs Thatcher's motion of No Confidence; but it naturally did little in the short run for the Labour Party's popularity in the country, or for that of the Liberals.

The difficulties of the government were compounded by the weakness of its extra-parliamentary organisation. The real membership was far less than the nominal total, because individual constituency parties were obliged to affiliate on a minimum figure (since 1961, one thousand) in order to obtain representation at Conference. The individual membership thus claimed in 1974 was almost 692,000, but the Houghton Committee on Financial Aid to Political Parties put it at an average of only 500 per constituency. This made it all the easier for small minorities, perhaps of the far Left, to capture a constituency general committee and then to eject a sitting M.P. The party's National Agent submitted a detailed report about the influence of the Militant group, a Trotskyist faction, but this was shelved by the National Executive, itself much to the Left of the parliamentary party; and in 1976 a member of the Militant group was actually appointed the party's Youth Officer. Early in 1977 the Executive finally decided to enquire into 'Entrism'—that is, the conspiratorial attempt to win control of its organs—but the enquiry soon ended with a plea for tolerance and the declaration that 'Trotskyist views cannot be beaten by disciplinary action.' It was true enough that the only clear case of a Labour M.P. being refused re-nomination by his management committee because of his right-wing attitude alone was Reg Prentice at Newham North-East, and in October 1977 he confirmed the views of his critics by resigning from the party and promptly joining the Conservatives.

But it was at this point that the government's fortunes were beginning to revive. By the summer of 1977 it was apparent that two years of the Social Contract had not merely limited wage increases substantially but had also made inroads into inflation. The T.U.C. could no longer hold back the demand for a return to collective bargaining, but Callaghan and Healey were not unsuccessful in insisting that the return should be 'orderly': that wage increases should take place only once a year and that they should be held as closely as possible to a maximum of 10 per cent. Government pressure was exerted to ensure that employers and unions observed these limits. At the same time, North Sea Oil was transforming the balance of payments and encouraging an upward movement of sterling, which also had a favourable effect on inflation. The Labour Party Conference at Brighton in early October was strangely cordial, considering the tensions that had only recently existed between left and right wings. By late October, the opinion polls suggested that Labour was as popular in the country as the Conservatives ; and so the prospects for a General Election in 1978 seemed altogether brighter.

(7)

The year 1978 was, on the whole, a year of economic recovery for Britain. The increase of output of North Sea Oil, as expected, turned the balance of payments from a deficit into a surplus. The pound was continuing to rise in value against other currencies, and inflation fell into single figures. Unemployment declined during the year, and general living standards rose by more than 8 per cent. But the government was still under heavy pressure in Parliament. It depended upon the support of the Liberal Party, and the Liberals, for their part, were disappointed by the policy concessions that they secured in return: for instance, the proposal to introduce proportional representation for the E.E.C. elections, which they strongly favoured, was opposed by four Cabinet ministers and most Labour M.P.s on a free vote in December 1977, and consequently defeated. In May 1978 David Steel, the Liberal leader, announced that his party would not continue the pact after the end of the session in July. By that date, the separate measures for devolution to both Scotland and Wales were on the Statute Book, although both had been amended to require not only an affirmative vote by referendum of the country concerned, but also approval by at least 40 per cent of the registered electors therein. Meanwhile, Labour's position in the opinion polls gave reason for hope, and a General Election in the autumn was widely expected.

To the surprise of most observers, Callaghan decided against an early dissolution. It was a mistaken decision, because his efforts to maintain some degree of wage restraint were already running into difficulties. He and Healey, the Chancellor, sought to establish a 5 per cent norm for settlements in 1978–9. Now that the rate of price inflation was dropping, the proposal was not unreasonable, for when a 10 per cent norm had been in operation, the actual increase in earnings had been of the order of 14 per cent. But both the Trades Union Congress and the Labour Party at their annual conferences demanded a return to free collective bargaining.

The result was what came to be called 'the winter of discontent'. It began with a two-month strike at Ford's where the result was an eventual settlement at about 15 per cent. The Government tried to impose penal sanctions on the company for being so generous, but this proposal was defeated in the Commons. A similar 15 per cent was given to B.B.C. technicians to prevent a blackout over Christmas. Then in January 1979 lorry drivers went on strike and engaged in militant action, including 'secondary picketing', that is, action designed to halt the movement of goods not directly involved in the original dispute. The Transport and General Workers Union eventually, in response to public pressure, drew up a 'code of practice' to avoid this misuse of picketing. But in addition to this, there were strikes by public service workers — ambulance men, water and sewerage workers, and municipal employees — which were very damaging to the unions' relations with the public: in the middle of a harsh winter, the roads were not gritted, and extra accidents undoubtedly occurred. An attempt to revive the social contract in the form of an annual 'national assessment' was derided by Mrs Thatcher as a 'boneless wonder'.

The pact with the Liberals having lapsed, the Government relied for survival on support from the Scottish and Welsh Nationalists. But on 1st March 1979 the referenda in Scotland and Wales were held, and they confounded the expectations of all on the Government side. In Scotland, although there was a small majority of the electorate in favour of devolution — 32.85 per cent to 30.78 — it was well short of the necessary 40 per cent; and in Wales the assembly proposal was turned down by more than four to one — 11.9 per cent to 46.9. On 28th March, on another vote of No Confidence, the Government, having lost the Scottish Nationalist support, was defeated by one vote. Callaghan was now forced to ask for an early dissolution of Parliament, and polling was fixed for 3rd May.

During this campaign Callaghan's avuncular style was more popular in the country than the rather abrasive style of Mrs Thatcher, and the Labour manifesto was much more moderate than the National Executive would have liked. A demand for the immediate abolition of the Lords, passed at the 1977 Conference, was dropped, and the only candidate for nationalisation was 'commercial ports and cargo handling'. But the work of the National Enterprise Board was to be extended, a wealth tax — left over from the previous Parliament — was to be introduced, and the system of comprehensive education was to be 'completed in the 1980s'. Public support of independent schools would be terminated. There were also to be higher pensions, more help for housing, and an improved health service, including free prescriptions once more.

Conservative policy seemed more relevant to the problems of the preceding winter. Trade union law was to be reformed in respect of picketing and the closed shop, and secret ballots for union decision-making were to be encouraged with public funds. Income tax was to be reduced, especially the 'absurdly high marginal rates of tax both at the bottom and top of the income scale'. Nationalisation would actually be reversed, by selling off aerospace and shipbuilding concerns, and by running down the National Enterprise Board. Between these policies and those of the Labour Party there was a sharp divide, and the Liberals, with their proposals for proportional representation, support for the E.E.C. and a transfer from direct to indirect taxation, made less impact.

The Labour organisation entered the election in poor shape. Party membership continued at a low level, and only 25 constituencies had as many as 1500 members each. The number of full-time agents had sunk to 70 — by no means all in marginal areas. Finance was also a bugbear, and a new body sponsored by David Basnett of the General and Municipal Workers, called 'Trade Unions for a Labour Victory' (set up in 1978), was regarded by many in the party as more of a diversion than an ally in raising funds. The Conservatives, on the other hand, were able to mount a lavish advertising campaign prepared by the new firm of Saatchi and Saatchi, and had well over 300 full-time agents.

In the upshot the Conservatives had a net gain of 55 seats and Labour a net loss of 40. The results were: Conservatives, 339; Labour, 269; Liberals, 11 (a loss of three). The Nationalist parties suffered severely: the Scottish Nationalists lost nine of their eleven seats, and the Welsh Nationalists one of three. The Labour vote, as a percentage of the total poll, sank from 39.2 to 36.9; the Conservative percentage rose from 35.8 to 43.9. But one feature of the results was the regional variation: in Southern England the swing from Labour to Conservative was as high as 7 per cent; in Scotland it was less than 1 per cent; and the national average was 5.2. The most prominent casualty on the Labour side was Shirley Williams, who was defending a seat in the London commuter area. On 4th May Callaghan resigned the Premiership, and the Queen invited Mrs Thatcher to form a new Conservative Government. Callaghan courteously offered his congratulations to the first woman Prime Minister that Britain had ever had: 'For a woman to occupy that office is a tremendous moment in the country's history'.

FURTHER READING

For Britain's accession to the Common Market in 1970–2, see U. Kitzinger, *Diplomacy and Persuasion* (1973). On the Industrial Relations Act, the best work so far is B. Weekes *et al.*, *Industrial Relations and the Limits of the Law* (Oxford,, 1975). For the Labour campaign against its enactment, see E. Heffer, *The Class Struggle in Parliament* (1973). The Lincoln by-election is described in C. Cook and J. Ramsden, *By-elections in British Politics* (1973). On the 1974 General Elections and on that of 1979 there are the usual Nuffield studies written jointly by D. E. Butler and D. Kavanagh. The report of Lord Houghton's committee, *Financial Aid to Political Parties* (Cmd. 6601, 1976), although not implemented, provides a valuable picture of the state of constituency organisation; Dianne Hayter, *The Labour Party: Crisis and Prospects* (Fabian Society, 1977) is also helpful. On the arrangement with the Liberal Party, see A. Michie and S. Hoggart, *The Pact* (1978). On the last Wilson Government, see Barbara Castle, *The Castle Diaries, 1974–76* (1980). The condition of the party just after the election of 1979 is well depicted in D. Kavanagh (ed.), *The Politics of the Labour Party* (1982).

CHAPTER XI

The S.D.P. Secession and the Dream Ticket (1979–84)

(1)

T H E General Election of May 1979 was followed a few weeks later, in June, by the first election of members of the European Parliament. For this purpose, the country was divided into only 81 seats, or 78 excluding Northern Ireland. So far as Labour was concerned, the results were very disappointing. Many supporters took the view that the European Parliament should be boycotted, and so there were widespread abstentions. The average poll was light, and Labour with only 33 per cent of the total took only 17 of the 78 British seats. Of the remainder, 60 were won by the Conservatives and one by a Scottish Nationalist. In these large constituencies the Liberals were unable to obtain a single seat. Barbara Castle was elected Leader of the Labour Group, which devoted itself to opposing increases in agricultural prices and to pressing for greater expenditure on regional and social policies.

Meanwhile on the reassembly of Parliament in May 1979 the Parliamentary Labour Party re-elected James Callaghan as Leader and Michael Foot as his deputy, both of them being unopposed. A dozen ex-Cabinet Ministers were elected to the Parliamentary Committee. Tony Benn had not stood for election, having decided to retire to the back benches so as to be free to criticise his erstwhile colleagues. As he was so much the spokesman of the National Executive majority, this was a bad sign for the future unity of the party.

It was not that there was any disagreement among Labour spokesmen about the harshness of the new Thatcher government's policies. Sir Geoffrey Howe, the new Chancellor of the Exchequer, fulfilled a campaign promise by cutting the standard rate of income tax from 33p to 30p, and reducing the top rate from 83p to 60p. But in order to raise the same amount of revenue, he increased Value Added Tax from 8 or 12½ per cent to a uniform 15 per cent. Healey said, not unjustifiably, that 'In ten minutes the Chancellor threw away the results of five years of hard, painstaking effort by the Labour Government in getting down inflation'. And, sure enough, by July the year-on-year index of retail prices was up to 15·6 per cent. The Chancellor's strict monetarist policies also meant a high rate of interest, just at the time when the pound was riding high in any case owing to the increased output of North Sea Oil. The result was to damage the export industries and to cause employers to dismiss workers. Unemployment rose rapidly throughout the year, and by the end of 1980 had reached 2¼ million.

Although the Labour Party could agree in condemning these policies, it could agree on little else. The National Executive majority favoured the policies of Tony Benn, who was supported by a grouping within the party called the Labour Co-ordinating Committee. Blaming Callaghan and Healey for the last government's failure, they sought constitutional reform of the party in order to make the leadership more directly responsible to the activists like themselves. Their proposals were threefold: to elect the Leader by the party organs at large rather than simply by the parliamentary party; to insist on the compulsory re-selection of M.P.s before a new General Election; and to transfer control of the election manifesto to the extra-parliamentary Executive itself. All these issues were debated at the Party Conference at Brighton in October 1979; and resolutions calling for mandatory re-selection of M.P.s and for Executive control of the manifesto were carried, although both had to await constitutional confirmation at the 1980 Conference. A resolution to broaden the basis for electing the Leader was, however, defeated. It was agreed 'overwhelmingly' to re-nationalise without compensation those sectors of industry which were denationalised by the Thatcher government. Finally, a commission was set up to enquire into party organisation and finance.

On 31st May 1980 a Special Conference was held at

Wembley to discuss a document which represented a compromise between factions within the party. It was entitled *Peace, Jobs, Freedom,* and was principally a criticism of the government's policies. But the day was marked by very cool receptions for Callaghan and Healey but exceptional enthusiasm for Benn. It was clear that the constituency delegates at least regarded him as their spokesman, and were tired of the older leadership of the party. He told the Conference that the Executive was working on a 'rolling manifesto' — that is to say, a party programme constantly in being, available for a general election at any time.

By the spring of 1980 the party headquarters had moved out of Transport House, where it had rented rooms from the Transport Workers ever since 1928. Its new offices were in the Walworth Road in south London, just beyond the Elephant and Castle. They were rented from a special Consortium of Trade Unions which had purchased the site and reconditioned the buildings. It was there that the Executive met to adopt its first edition of the 'rolling manifesto'. This called for unilateral nuclear disarmament, abolition of the House of Lords, and further substantial extensions of public ownership. A radical reform of the Common Agricultural Policy was to be a precondition of continued membership of the Common Market.

The 1980 Party Conference met at Blackpool. The balance of union voting had changed somewhat, the Engineering Workers having joined the opponents of change: and this resulted in the defeat of a call for Executive control of the election manifesto. But by a small majority the mandatory re-selection of M.P.s was endorsed, and it was agreed to elect the party leader by means of an electoral college, the details of its composition being left over for decision at a further special one-day conference in January 1981. Unilateral nuclear disarmament was approved overwhelmingly, but a call for withdrawal from the North Atlantic Treaty Organisation was rejected. The Conference also accepted, with some misgivings, the only coherent recommendation to emerge from the Commission of Enquiry, namely, an increase of subscriptions.

Neil Kinnock (b. 1942) and Michael Foot (b. 1913)

Shortly after the end of the Conference, Callaghan re-signed the party leadership, and a new election took place by the old methods, that is to say, by a ballot of the parliamentary party. Tony Benn refused to stand, saying that he preferred to wait until the new method of election had come into operation. In the first ballot, Denis Healey secured 112 votes, Michael Foot 83, John Silkin 38, and Peter Shore 32. Silkin and Shore, having been eliminated, both backed Foot; and Foot was elected Leader on 10th November, having won 139 votes in the second ballot to Healey's 129. At 67, Foot was only sixteen months younger than Callaghan, and had had much less experience of government. It was the first time since Lansbury that a man clearly identified with the Left had been elected Leader. Although somewhat tempered in his views by membership of the Wilson and Callaghan Cabinets, he was nevertheless still a unilateral disarmer and an opponent of the Common Market. The more right-wing M.P.s probably saw him as a convenient caretaker; and Denis Healey was elected unopposed as his deputy. The parliamentary party also elected a pre-dominantly right-wing Shadow Cabinet, although William Rodgers, who was one of those elected, was dissatisfied with the post that he was offered and decided to serve 'at large'.

(2)

Rodgers was one of those most discontented with the shift to the Left within the party. He, with David Owen and Shirley Williams — the latter not an M.P. but still a member of the National Executive — had announced in June that they would leave the party if it adopted withdrawal from the Common Market as party policy. They were dubbed 'the Gang of Three', on the analogy of Chinese politics. But they were already in touch with another leading ex-minister of earlier Labour governments, Roy Jenkins, who was due to return at the end of the year from his tour of duty as President of the European Commission in Brussels. Jenkins had already broken with the Labour

Party when he delivered the Dimbleby Lecture on B.B.C. television in November 1979. He had called for the revival of the 'radical centre' in British politics, but seemed unwilling to commit himself to the Liberal Party.

On 24th January 1981 the special Labour Party Conference to consider the precise make-up of the electoral college for the leadership election met at Wembley. It decided in favour of giving the trade unions 40 per cent of the votes, and the constituency parties and the parliamentary party 30 per cent each. Next day the 'Gang of Three' met with Roy Jenkins at David Owen's house and issued what they called the 'Limehouse Declaration', which asserted: 'We believe that the need for a realignment of British politics must now be faced'. Thereupon the newspapers spoke of the 'Gang of Four', and the group advertised in the *Guardian* for the support of the public. They at once secured a substantial response, together with financial contributions on a generous scale.

The formation of the new Social Democratic Party took place in March. It was hastened by the interest taken by the press and the public, which was reflected in the opinion polls. A poll in mid-March, for instance, showed the Social Democrats already securing 30 per cent of the total vote, a figure surpassing that of any of the other parties. As yet this could be no more than an expression of hostility to the latter, for the Social Democrats had no policy of their own, and seemed to be especially strong among the middle-aged and middle-class elements of the population. Shirley Williams and Tom Bradley, a trade-union colleague, had resigned their seats on the Labour Party's National Executive in February; and when the party was formed in March altogether 13 M.P.s resigned the Labour whip to join. One Conservative M.P., Christopher Brocklebank-Fowler of Norfolk North-West, did likewise. It was not at all clear how well the new party would fare when faced with the electorate of a working-class constituency: but Roy Jenkins bravely put this to the test at Warrington in July, and scored a moral victory by polling 42·4 per cent of the vote in a seat where Labour had had a majority of over 10,000. Later in the summer the Social

Democrats and Liberals agreed to an alliance to avoid rival candidatures in future contests.

Meanwhile in the spring Tony Benn declared his intention of standing for the post of deputy leader of the Labour Party. Michael Foot was averse to this as he foresaw a prolonged struggle between Benn and Healey to win the votes of the constituency parties and the trade unions — almost like an American presidential election. He invited Benn to contest the leadership against himself. But Benn persisted in his plan, and the result was that he and Healey were in contention throughout the summer. In the glare of media publicity, it became apparent that the methods of many of the trade unions for assessing the views of their members were arbitrary to say the least. The campaign came to its climax with the voting on the Sunday before the party conference met at Brighton in late September 1981. Healey was re-elected by the narrow margin of 50·4 per cent to 49·6. Over four-fifths of the constituency parties had voted for Benn, but Healey had secured two-thirds of both the trade unions and the parliamentary party. The conference itself reflected a certain shift to the right among the unions, in that several left-wing members of the Executive were defeated, and control reverted instead to the more moderate Left represented by Michael Foot himself. But a resolution in favour of withdrawal from the Common Market without a fresh referendum was carried by a large majority.

The immediate defection of more Labour M.P.s to the Social Democratic Party was almost certainly averted by Healey's success. But, considering the lamentable state of the economy by this time, with some three million unemployed, and also the strong revival of the unilateral disarmament campaign, the Labour Party's failure in by-elections could not but be alarming. At Croydon North-West in late October a Liberal candidate, standing with Social-Democrat support, was elected with 40 per cent of the vote, and the Labour vote dropped from 40 per cent to 26 per cent. Another contest followed at Crosby in Lancashire: the seat had been held by the Conservatives in 1979 with a majority of over 19,000, but Shirley Williams, standing for the new centre alliance, won an easy victory, while the Labour candidate lost his deposit. By the end of 1981 a total of 23 Labour M.P.s had joined the new party; and on 25 March 1982 Roy Jenkins won a Conservative seat at a by-election at Glasgow, Hillhead, and thus returned to Parliament to lead the group, which a year later numbered 29 in all.

(3)

Only a few days after Jenkins's by-election victory, however, on 2 April 1982, the political situation was transformed by the sudden Argentinian invasion of the Falkland Islands. The Government had been at fault in not anticipating this move; and Lord Carrington, the Foreign Secretary, felt obliged to resign office. But a great majority of M.P.s of all parties at once agreed that Britain now had a moral duty to restore the status quo in a Crown Colony, and Michael Foot, denouncing the Argentinian Government as 'fascist', supported the despatch of a task force of warships and troops to the South Atlantic to secure this end. The Argentinian junta proved obdurate, in spite of attempts by the American Secretary of State, Alexander Haig, to mediate. Hostilities began in earnest on 3 May when, on orders from London, a British submarine torpedoed an Argentinian cruiser, the *General Belgrano*, with heavy loss of life. The task force in turn suffered loss at the hands of the Argentinian air force, but effected a landing on the main island which led to a rapid advance towards the main enemy positions at Port Stanley.

On 14 June the Argentinian forces, although numerically superior, capitulated; altogether 255 British servicemen and civilians had been killed. Henceforward for many months the 'Falklands factor' counted in favour of Mrs Thatcher and the Conservative Party in public opinion and at by-elections. In July an opinion poll showed the Conservative Party with 46.5 per cent support, as against 27.5 per cent for Labour and 24 per cent for the Liberal-S.D.P. Alliance.

Labour's political recovery was hindered by its own continuing internal dissension. Several sitting M.P.s were rejected by the re-selection procedure, and at Bermondsey Robert Mellish, the former Chief Whip, who was facing this fate, resigned from the party in August and announced his intention of shortly resigning his seat. In June the National Executive had already approved a recommendation from the party secretariat to treat the Militant group as a 'party within a party' and hence contrary to the constitution. This recommendation was approved by the Blackpool Party Conference in October by a large majority and, in December, after the Militant leaders had lost an appeal to the High Court, the National Executive reaffirmed its decision against what Foot had described at the conference as 'a pestilential nuisance.'

The unions at the Party Conference of 1982 were willing to support the 'soft left' — that is to say, Michael Foot and his immediate followers — but showed little sympathy for the 'hard left', which dominated the constituency parties, and whose most prominent spokesman was Tony Benn. The conference carried overwhelmingly a vote for unilateral nuclear disarmament, but narrowly defeated a call for the nationalisation of all banks. While rejecting interference with free collective bargaining, it accepted the idea of a 'national economic assessment' to guide wage settlements in agreement with the T.U.C. The Thatcher Government had found a solution of sorts for wage inflation through heavy unemployment: there was, however, no noticeable economic recovery, and those out of work numbered over three million throughout the year. Several usually militant unions, including even the miners, rejected strike calls from their executives; and inflation dropped from 12 per cent in January to 5.4 per cent in December.

In late February 1983 Mellish's by-election took place: the normally safe working-class constituency of Bermondsey suddenly returned a Liberal candidate with an overwhelming majority. Peter Tatchell, the young Labour candidate, was a member of the 'hard left', though not actually a Militant supporter; but he also suffered from an exceptionally hostile press because he was an open homosexual. Labour's confidence in its heartlands was revived in March, however, when a strong local candidate won the somewhat marginal seat of Darlington, and at the local elections early in May the two main contenders were still clearly the Conservatives and Labour, with Labour making only a few gains, but emerging with control of two-thirds of the 36 English metropolitan district councils.

(4)

Only a few days after the results of the local elections were declared, Mrs Thatcher declared her decision to dissolve Parliament and hold a General Election on 9 June. Michael Foot called it a 'cut-and-run election', and it is possible that she felt that Conservative popularity might have waned by the autumn. The Labour manifesto, adopted on 11 May and entitled *The New Hope for Britain*, was an ambiguous document: on disarmament, it said that 'Unilateralism and multilateralism must go hand in hand if either is to succeed'; and on the Common Market:

> British withdrawal from the Community is the right policy for Britain — to be completed within the lifetime of the Parliament. But we are also committed to bring about withdrawal in an amicable and orderly way, so that we do not prejudice employment.

It did, however, clearly call for a rapid expansion of state spending, with the object of bringing unemployment below one million within five years. The Conservatives in their manifesto promised fresh legislation to reduce the powers of trade unions and to abolish the metropolitan councils; they also undertook to continue the sale of nationalised industries to private buyers.

The trade unions had been affronted by the Thatcher Government's restriction of their powers and immunities already made by the Employment Acts of 1980 and 1982. Many of the larger unions got together to form a new body called 'Trade Unions for a Labour Victory', which was designed simultaneously to give the unions more control over the use to which their political funds were put. How far the party benefited directly from this is not clear, but the usual General Election Fund was above its target at substantially over £2 million. This, however, could not make up for the shortage of full-time agents, whose number had now sunk to only 63, as against the Conservatives' 320. It was an unequal contest: throughout the campaign the opinion polls showed the Conservatives well in the lead, and the only change was that the Alliance, which had been a poor third, crept up on Labour as polling-day approached. Labour's disunity on defence was evident when Denis Healey said that a Labour Government would renounce Polaris (the submarines armed with nuclear weapons) only 'if we get adequate concessions from the Soviet Union'; and James Callaghan emphasised that 'Polaris submarines . . . have a further life span of ten to twelve years, and perhaps longer as effective weapons.' When Healey, referring to the Falklands campaign, said that Mrs Thatcher 'glories in slaughter', he was rebuked by the widow of Colonel H. Jones, V.C., one of the campaign's heroes, and was obliged to withdraw his remark.

It is difficult to compare the election results with those of 1979, not only because of the stronger challenge from the third party, but also because of the redistribution of seats which had taken place. The total size of the House was enlarged from 635 members to 650. But the scale of the Conservative triumph was not in doubt. There were 397 Conservative M.P.s in the new Commons, a gain of 65 since the dissolution, as against 209 for Labour — a loss of 29 and the lowest figure since before the 1945 election. The Alliance secured a vote not far below Labour's, but won only 23 seats, of which 17 were Liberal and 6 S.D.P.: this was a net gain of 4 Liberal seats and a net loss of 23 for the S.D.P. Tony Benn was defeated in a new and marginal seat at Bristol, and Shirley Williams lost her newly-won seat at Crosby. The Conservative vote was just over 13 million, or 42 per cent of the total turnout — slightly less than in 1979. But Labour was down to just under 8½ million, or 27.6 per cent; and the Alliance secured 7¾ million, or 25.4 per cent. The Labour vote went down by an average of 9.5 per cent, and the party lost 119 deposits. As the Conservative vote had also fallen, the swing from Labour to Conservative may be calculated as 3.9 per cent. There were now no Labour M.P.s in the Southern or South-Eastern Regions of England and only one in the South-West. Portsmouth, from where the task force had largely set forth, showed a 9 per cent swing to the Conservatives; on the other hand, Merseyside, suffering from acute unemployment, swung towards Labour and elected two more Labour M.P.s. Proportionately, of course, the heaviest losses in seats were suffered by the S.D.P., which lost two of the original 'Gang of Four' — Bill Rodgers as well as Shirley Williams — and almost all its followers. Although the Alliance came second in no less than 309 seats it had failed to 'break the mould' as Roy Jenkins had hoped.

(5)

The election was followed almost immediately by an announcement from Michael Foot that he would retire from the leadership at the following party conference. Denis Healey also gave up his post as deputy leader. Within hours there was talk of a 'dream ticket' combining two of the younger members of the party leadership, one of the 'soft Left', like Foot himself, and the other more right-wing: these were Neil Kinnock, a Welshman — albeit of Scottish origin — representing the new seat of Islwyn, who was aged 41; and Roy Hattersley, who had been Secretary for Prices and Consumer Protection in 1976–9, and who was a Yorkshireman aged 50 representing a Birmingham seat. The two of them, it was thought, would reunite the party; and since Kinnock had never served in the Cabinet, he was free of any blame attaching to the last Labour Government. Within a fortnight the Transport and General Workers, having put the issue to their biennial conference, decided to nominate Kinnock as leader; and thereafter he remained ahead in the campaign, with older leaders such as Peter Shore and Eric Heffer securing very little support. When the annual conference met at Brighton in early October, balloting took place under the new procedure. Kinnock was well ahead of

186

Hattersley, his nearest rival for the leadership, and secured large majorities in all three categories — trade unions, constituency parties and parliamentary party. Hattersley then secured a similar success for the deputy leadership over the other principal contender, Michael Meacher, a left-winger who had relative youth on his side —he was 44 — but who would not have balanced the team.

The conference gave a great welcome to its new leader, and there seemed to be a widespread desire for an end to feuding and for a fresh start. It was recognised that the programme on which the party had fought the election had not appealed to the voters. The new party secretary, Jim Mortimer, who was well-suited for his task, having served a term as chairman of the Advisory, Conciliation and Arbitration Service, declared that unpopular policies and disunity rather than faults of organisation had been responsible for the electoral defeat. Hattersley said that the unequivocal pledge to withdraw from the E.E.C. 'was wrong in principle and lost us votes.' The conference also finally confirmed the expulsion of the five staff members of the *Militant* newspaper. But left-wing feeling was still strong in the constituency parties, which re-elected Tony Benn to the Executive at the top of the poll and also two left-wing newcomers, Michael Meacher, and David Blunkett, the blind leader of Sheffield City Council.

When the new parliamentary party met in October, however, it transpired that its views did not differ all that significantly from the old. Denis Healey, Gerald Kaufman and Peter Shore, who had all been prominent in the Callaghan administration, turned up as the top three in the Shadow Cabinet elections. When Kinnock allotted Shadow Cabinet responsibilities, therefore, apart from assigning Hattersley to the Treasury, he had to accept Denis Healey as Foreign Affairs spokesman and Kaufman for Home Affairs. Peter Shore was to look after Trade and Industry and also serve as Shadow Leader of the House. The team was selected in the absence of Tony Benn from the House: he did not return until he won a by-election at Chesterfield in March 1984.

Although Mortimer had not blamed party organisation as

the principal factor in the party's electoral defeat, he did not conceal the fact that there were some very serious organisational weaknesses. These persisted after the election, and the party headquarters faced a cash crisis owing to the refusal of the trade unions to raise their affiliation payments. The unions had been hit hard by the depression in industry; and their support for the party was threatened in any case by the Government's proposal to introduce a third trade-union reform bill, which would oblige them to hold ballots on political affiliation at least every ten years. The members of twelve of the 68 unions presently paying the political levy had reported that more than half their members were contracted out. It was likely, therefore, that ballots in these cases would go against affiliation, and that other unions might also be lost to the party. Len Murray, the T.U.C. secretary, managed to persuade Tom King, the new Secretary for Employment, not to insist on the re-introduction of contracting-in, although only by promising fuller publicity by the unions to their members of the procedure for contracting-out. For a time in the spring on 1984 the new Kinnock-Hattersley leadership appeared to enjoy a 'honeymoon' success by temporarily putting the Labour Party into the lead in the opinion polls; but by the time of the Blackpool Conference in the autumn this lead had disappeared, probably owing to widespread concern at the violence engendered by the prolonged miners' strike and the ambivalence of many in the party to it.

FURTHER READING

There is a good short biography of *Michael Foot* by Simon Hoggart and David Leigh (1979). The struggle between the supporters of Tony Benn and their opponents within the Labour Party may best be traced in the pages of the party's publication, the *Labour Weekly*. On the emergence of the Social Democratic Party see Ian Bradley, *Breaking the Mould?* (1981). For the views of Tony Benn, see his *Arguments for Democracy* (1981). A Fabian pamphlet by David Webster, *The Labour Party and the New Left* (1981) is useful for distinguishing the elements in the coalition of forces supporting Mr Benn. See also Patrick Seyd, *The Rise and Fall of the Labour Left* (1987) and Michael Crick, *Militant* (1984). On the election, see D. E. Butler and D. Kavanagh, *British General Election of 1983* (1984). See also David and Maurice Kogan, *The Battle for the Labour Party* (1982).

CHAPTER XII

Revival under Kinnock

(1985-92)

(1)

THE late 1980s saw a marked recovery of the party's standing in the country, giving it in late 1989 a lead of 10 per cent in the opinion polls. This was due to four interlocking factors, and it is difficult to distinguish which was most important. There was, first of all, a determination on the part of the new leadership of the party to secure unity of purpose. Secondly, the Liberal–Social Democrat Alliance disintegrated after the 1987 General Election, in which it had lost some ground. Thirdly, the Government's economic policy led at the end of the decade to a return of inflation, high mortgage rates and the prospect of renewed recession. And fourthly, the Government introduced a highly unpopular uniform 'poll tax' in place of rates. But when the new General Election took place in April 1992, Mrs Thatcher had gone, there was a new Conservative leader, and a fourth consecutive Conservative victory.

(2)

Neil Kinnock gradually asserted his control of the National Executive and of the party in the country, as was shown by successive votes both at the Executive's monthly meetings and at the annual Conferences. He was powerfully aided by a new General Secretary roughly of his own age — Larry Whitty, a Cambridge graduate who had been a trade union research officer. A still younger man, Peter Mandelson, a grandson of Herbert Morrison, was appointed Director of Campaigns and Communications — a new post. This was a team that augured well for the future.

Kinnock had first to deal with the 'hard left' in the country, and especially in local councils such as Liverpool and Lambeth. It was true that left-wing councils were also targeted by the Conservative Government, which imposed 'rate-capping' measures to limit their expenditure. But Kinnock could not approve attempts to defy 'rate-capping', which led to councillors being suspended and surcharged. He and his colleagues vigorously resisted a Government measure to abolish the Greater London Council and the Metropolitan Councils, which was nevertheless carried into law in July 1985.

In effect Kinnock was having to fight on two fronts at the same time, dissociating himself as far as he could from what was known in the media as the 'loony left' but also maintaining the assault upon the Government. In his keynote speech at the Bournemouth Conference in 1985, he made a vigorous attack on the Militant control of the Liverpool City Council. But he already knew that the Conference was backing him by electing a National Executive more to his liking by placing Tony Benn and his followers in a small minority. A call for 'black sections' of local parties to be given constitutional status was resisted, but the National Executive agreed to establish a Black and Asian Advisory Committee; this however proved inadequate to satisfy black aspirations.

Hanging over the party's finances was the threat posed by the 1984 Employment Act, which required the affiliated unions to re-ballot their members on the issue of political funds. Since in some unions the number of those contributing was small, it was expected that there would be a contraction in the number of unions retaining such funds. However, after a carefully organised campaign emphasising the need for the unions to be free to take political action, all the unions which already had political funds voted to retain them, and several other unions voted to establish them. In April 1986 the National Executive passed a vote of thanks to the organisers of this campaign, Bill Keys of the Graphical and Allied Trades and Graham Allen of the Transport and General Workers.

Meanwhile the Alliance of Liberals and Social Democrats continued to do well in by-elections, and it was not until April 1986 that Labour was able to gain a seat from the Conservatives, at Fulham. In the spring and summer of that year the National Executive had to spend much of its time on the issue of the expulsion of the Liverpool Militants. After the Militants resorted to the courts, and secured a judgment limiting the powers of the Executive to take summary action, Whitty proposed that the party establish a disciplinary system separate from the Executive; this was approved at the 1986 Conference by a large majority, under the title of 'National Constitutional Committee'. That Conference also, by a large majority, confirmed the expulsion of the Liverpool Militant leaders. Kinnock, in his address to the Conference, spoke not of nationalisation but of 'social ownership', including co-operatives, municipal enterprises and a National Investment Bank. He affirmed his support for the North Atlantic Treaty Organisation, but on atomic weapons he re-asserted his faith in unilateral disarmament: 'I would fight and die for my country, but I tell you I would not let my country die for me'. It was agreed that there should be at least one woman on every parliamentary constituency short list; but in the process of re-selection only six sitting M.P.s who sought reselection were denied it.

Early in 1987 it was still not clear that Labour, rather than the Alliance, would be the main challenger to the Conservatives at the coming General Election. In February the Social Democratic Party won a by-election at Greenwich, a formerly safe Labour seat, and this clearly posed a threat to Labour prospects in the south of England. The Budget in the spring proposed a 2p reduction in income tax and no increases in beer or tobacco taxes. After the local elections in early May, which gave some encouragement to the Conservatives, Mrs Thatcher secured a dissolution of Parliament and a General Election on 11 June.

The Labour manifesto, entitled *Britain Will Win*, concentrated on a campaign to increase employment — the jobless total was still over three million — and to maintain the National Health Service and public education. Some of the more radical proposals of 1983 had been dropped, such as abolishing the House of Lords, withdrawing from the Common Market, and closing down the American nuclear bases. But the party was still vulnerable on defence, being committed to the decommissioning of the British nuclear deterrent, a proposal which opinion polls showed was not popular in the country.

Nevertheless, aided by the most modern public relations techniques available, Labour fought a vigorous campaign. A Campaign Management Team was appointed; it decided to give special prominence to Neil Kinnock and his attractive wife, Glenys, in television broadcasts. The symbol used to accompany them was not the red flag but the red rose. In London Bryan Gould, an agreeably bland New Zealander, acted as campaign coordinator. A week before polling day, on the evidence of a rogue poll, Mrs Thatcher grew seriously concerned about the success of the Labour campaign, while the Alliance leaders, David Steel and David Owen, found themselves at odds over how they would act in the event of a 'hung' or balanced Parliament.

The result was nowhere near a hung Parliament. For the Conservatives it was not far from being a repetition of their success in 1983. In fact they secured a slightly higher overall poll, at 46.2 per cent, as against 46.0 per cent four years earlier. But their score in seats was 375, as against 397 before. Labour's recovery to 29.5 per cent, as against 26.9 per cent, was largely at the expense of the Alliance, whose vote dropped from 26.4 per cent to 23.8 per cent. There was a net gain to Labour of 20 seats, bringing their total to 229, including four seats for black or Asian candidates. The Alliance won 22 seats, one less than before. The Conservatives had an overall majority of 102, the second largest majority since 1945; but the national picture concealed some remarkable regional variations. The Conservatives lost half of their remaining seats in Scotland and now had no representation in several big Northern cities — Glasgow, Newcastle, Manchester, and Bradford. Labour, on the other hand, was woefully weak in southern England, having actually lost ground in London; and the main challenger in three-fifths of Conservative-held seats was still the Alliance. The proportion of trade-union members who had voted Labour had increased somewhat, from 39 per cent in 1983 to 42 per cent; but trade-union membership as a proportion of the electorate had dropped from 30 per cent to 23 per cent.

When the new Shadow Cabinet was chosen by Kinnock after the re-assembly of Parliament, his hands were freed by the retirement of Denis Healey and Peter Shore to the back benches. Roy Hattersley moved from being Shadow Chancellor to Home Affairs, John Smith replacing him in the Treasury post and Gerald Kaufman taking Healey's place in shadowing the Foreign Secretary. Bryan Gould, after his prominence in the election campaign, was rewarded with Trade and Industry; and for the first time a Shadow Minister for Women's Rights was appointed — Jo Richardson. The Annual Conference in the autumn met in somewhat chastened mood, there being a general realisation that the party's election programme had been out of step with the mood of the electorate. The Conference agreed to 'initiate a review of the Party's policies', the review to be reported to the Conference in 1988. It was also accepted that the selection or re-selection of candidates for Parliament should be effected by a college system, with the trade unions and other affiliated bodies having a maximum of 40 per cent of the votes. John Evans, speaking for the National Executive, revealed that at the selection conferences before the general election 'in almost one-third of the constituencies ... less than 30 people were in attendance to select the parliamentary candidate'.

Meanwhile David Steel, disappointed by the result of the Alliance campaign in the general election, had decided to force the issue of a merger of the Liberal and Social Democrats. A referendum of the two parties was held and each returned a majority in favour of a merger; but David Owen, the S.D.P. leader, disagreed, as did two of their other four M.P.s. The Labour Party could not but gain from these ructions, especially as disappointment was growing with the Government's economic policy. Although Nigel Lawson, the Chancellor of the Exchequer, pleased the City in his 1988 Budget by reducing income tax to two simple rates of 25 per cent and 40 per cent, he was obliged to raise interest rates in the summer to 10 per cent and could not prevent inflation from rising to 5.9 per cent in September.

The 1988 Conference at Blackpool, therefore, found the Labour Party in more confident mood. A challenge from Tony Benn for the leadership and from Eric Heffer and John Prescott for the deputy leadership were easily seen off by Kinnock and Hattersley. Kinnock won 88.6 per cent of the vote against Benn, and this included three-quarters of the constituency parties. The success was in spite of a move on Kinnock's part away from commitment to unilateral disarmament — a move made easier by the readiness of the new Soviet leader Mikhail Gorbachev to agree to bilateral disarmament with the United States. In June Kinnock had said 'We want to get rid of Trident [the Government's new submarine-mounted nuclear weapon being bought from the United States]. But the fact is that it does not have to be something for nothing'. This statement led to the resignation of Labour's Defence spokesman, Denzil Davies.

The reports of the Policy Review Groups presented to the Conference rejected old-fashioned nationalisation in favour of 'social ownership' of natural monopolies and offered a compromise statement on defence which was to be expanded in the following year. They were overwhelmingly approved. Against the advice of the platform, however, a resolution in favour of unilateralism was carried with the help of the block vote of the Transport Workers, though not by any large majority. A potentially important decision was taken to recruit party members centrally instead of merely through the branches: and the Conference also agreed that at least one woman should appear on every constituency short list.

In May 1989 the National Executive approved and published its new policies, which excluded even 'social ownership' except for British Telecom and the water industry — the latter about to be privatised by the Government. The three Trident submarines likely to be completed by the time Labour could take office were to be a 'bargaining chip' for disarmament negotiations and not immediately scrapped. There was also to be a more positive attitude to the Common Market, following the appearance of Jacques Delors, the President of the European Commission, at the 1988 T.U.C. Conference and his promise of a 'Social Charter' to guarantee workers' rights.

In the spring, although unemployment continued to decline, and by April was below the 2 million mark, inflation had reached 7.5 per cent and mortgage rates reached 13 per cent. Labour re-emerged in the lead in the opinion polls, and in May won a by-election in a Conservative seat, the Vale of Glamorgan. In June, after a rather lukewarm Conservative campaign, Labour won an overall victory in the European elections, gaining 45 seats as against 32 for the Conservatives and one for the Scottish Nationalists. The Alliance, now reshaped as the 'Social and Liberal Democrats', as before were unable to win a seat and in terms of votes fell to fourth place below the Green Party, which, although also unable to win a seat, made a sudden surge to secure 15 per cent of the total vote.

The 1989 Conference of the party held at Brighton was free of the bitterness which had animated previous Conferences. It approved the policy reviews and elected a new Executive still more favourable to Kinnock than its predecessor. John Edmonds, the secretary of the General, Municipal and Boilermakers Union, proposed and carried a resolution in favour of reducing the weight of the block vote in decision-making, detailed proposals to be made by the Executive and presented to the 1990 Conference. The party's individual membership was expected to rise in any case as a result of the 1988 decision to allow the party head office to recruit members, and because of the reduction of the individual subscription rate for trade unionists belonging to affiliated unions.

The new parliamentary session for 1989–90 began with Labour in confident mood and the Conservatives in some disarray. Mrs Thatcher had decided in the summer to replace her Foreign Secretary, Sir Geoffrey Howe, who now became Deputy Prime Minister; in the autumn, as a result of disagreement over economic policy, her Chancellor of the Exchequer, Nigel Lawson, resigned, to be replaced by the new Foreign Secretary, John Major. The rise in inflation provoked a series of strikes in public sector occupations, culminating in a long struggle with the ambulance workers, who retained a good deal of public sympathy. When Parliament re-assembled in the autumn, the elections for the Shadow

Cabinet confirmed Kinnock's control over his party. For the first time members were asked to vote for three places reserved for women; this increased the total number (apart from Kinnock and Hattersley) from fifteen to eighteen. The first five places were, however, won by men, namely, Gordon Brown, John Smith (both of whom had won their spurs in attacking Nigel Lawson), Robin Cook (spokesman for the Health Service), Tony Blair (who now took on Employment) and Gerald Kaufman (Foreign Affairs). The top three were all Scots, who constituted almost a quarter of the entire parliamentary party.

But the very fact of Mrs Thatcher's relative weakness at this time — she even had to face for the first time a challenge to her position from inside her own party, though it was easily defeated — meant that she was not likely to risk an early general election. At the same time this also gave Labour more time to complete the review of its policies and the revision of its constitution. On the policy front, the salience of defence was much reduced at a time when in Europe the Iron Curtain of the post-war settlement was disintegrating. So far as the party constitution was concerned, Kinnock was at one with Edmonds in regarding the block vote as an embarrassment. A striking example of its impact was shown in December 1989, when a particularly able if occasionally maverick M.P., Frank Field, was denied re-selection, not by the majority of local members in his constituency, Birkenhead, but by the block vote of the Transport Workers. His difficulties were only finally resolved after a further selection meeting ordered by the National Executive.

In August Saddam Hussein, the dictator of Iraq, invaded and claimed to annex the small but oil-rich neighbouring state of Kuwait. This led to a United Nations' decision to restore Kuwait to independence and hence to the despatch under American leadership of a large expeditionary force to Saudi Arabia. The collapse of Soviet Russia enabled the one remaining superpower, the United States, to secure United Nations' support for its intervention, at the head of a coalition to which Britain, France and other Arab states made important contributions. On this issue the Labour Party was almost entirely in support of the Government. In the event, after an ultimatum to Saddam to withdraw expired on 15 January 1991, a short campaign, mostly of air attacks, led to the rapid collapse of the Iraqi forces. The war was over by the end of February. Allied casualties were light, and only 24 British servicemen were killed. But Saddam Hussein was not removed from power and remained a disturbing influence in the Middle East.

Meanwhile the Labour Party Conference at Blackpool in 1990 had agreed to support several constitutional changes, to take effect after the next general election. One of them was the establishment of a 'Black and Asian Socialist Society' with a representative on the National Executive. Another was mandatory quotas for women at various levels of the party. Yet a third was a proposal for the selection of parliamentary candidates on the basis of one member one vote, which meant a reduction of trade-union influence at that level. All these proposals were referred to the National Executive for constitutional formulation.

In November 1990, by an astonishing internal convulsion, Mrs Thatcher was removed from the leadership of the Conservative Party. This was owing to the hostility of her colleagues to her anti-European views, and to general dissatisfaction with the community charge or 'poll tax', which had replaced the rates and was proving difficult to enforce. Her successor was John Major, who had only entered the Commons in 1979 and only served in the Cabinet for three years. At 47, he was the youngest of the three party leaders. A sudden surge of support for the new Prime Minister put the Conservatives back in the lead in the opinion polls.

No doubt he was tempted to call an immediate general election. But he preferred to seek to put his own stamp on the political scene first. He proposed a 'citizens' charter' to guarantee the rights of consumers against the big monopolies such as the railways and the hospitals. In December he went to a conference of the European Community at

Maastricht and by a skilful balancing act managed to secure Britain's freedom to opt out of both the single European currency and the social charter. He was thus able to prevent the issue of European federalism from dominating politics in the run-up to the British general election.

(4)

The forthcoming election dominated the politics of the early months of 1992. In early March Norman Lamont, Major's successor as Chancellor, presented a Budget which was clearly designed with election strategy in view. He proposed a 20p tax band for the first £2,000 of taxable income (instead of 25p), but also postulated a borrowing requirement of no less than £28 billion. Meanwhile, the Environment Secretary, Michael Heseltine, was undertaking the replacement of the poll tax with a reversion to a rating system. The general election was called for 9 April, as had been widely predicted.

The Labour manifesto was entitled *Time to get Britain working again.* It advocated increased public investment in housing, public transport and education, and tax credits for research and development in industry. Scotland was to have an elected Parliament; Wales an elected Assembly; and English local government was to be reformed with a new 'regional tier' which would 'later form the basis for elected regional governments'. There would be a Ministry for Women, and race-discrimination laws would be strengthened. Labour would 'retain Britain's nuclear capability' while other nations did likewise, but not increase it. It was also intended within five years to reach the United Nations' target of providing 0.7 per cent of the gross national product for overseas aid. A party committee under Professor Raymond Plant would study alternative-voting systems, and make recommendations.

During the campaign, the Conservatives argued that Labour's programme could not be achieved without a massive increase in taxation. To counter this, John Smith

John Smith (b. 1938)

produced a 'shadow budget' to replace that of Lamont: he proposed to increase direct taxation only for those earning £36,375 or more, but acknowledged that the £21,000 upper limit on national insurance contributions would also have to go. It is not clear whether the campaign made much difference to the result: the opinion polls regularly pointed to a Labour lead, or at worst a 'hung' Parliament, in which no party would gain a majority.

The final outcome, therefore, was a surprise to almost all observers—except perhaps John Major himself and the Conservative campaign manager, Chris Patten. The Conservatives returned with 336 seats, giving them a majority of nineteen over all other parties. Labour's total rose to 271, having registered 44 gains and one loss. The Liberal Democrats (as they were now called) with 20 seats and the Scottish Nationalists with three seats made no advance, though Plaid Cymru gained one seat, to a total of four. In percentage terms of the total vote, comparing Conservatives with Labour, there had been a swing of only 1.9 to Labour, which still needed an extra 3.9 to match the Conservatives. The reasons for the failure of the opinion polls to predict the results accurately were much debated. It was clear that the Conservative success in securing their fourth electoral victory in a row was very damaging to the Labour Party.

After the result was known, Neil Kinnock at once decided to resign his post as leader; Roy Hattersley promptly also decided to retire; and Gerald Kaufman left the shadow Cabinet. A special conference to elect a new leadership was convened for 18 July. The principal candidate to emerge was John Smith, who was actually three and a half years older than Kinnock, and had served briefly in the Callaghan Cabinet. Margaret Beckett, his deputy in the existing Treasury team, but with a more left-wing background, offered herself for the post of deputy leader. But they did not go unchallenged: Bryan Gould stood for both posts, and John Prescott for the deputy leadership. Owing to the expense involved, many of the unions did not ballot their members, but their consultations soon showed that Smith would win the contest. In the event, Smith gained 91 per cent of the vote at the special conference, with sweeping majorities in each category — M.P.s, trade unions and constituency Labour parties. Mrs Beckett also won handsomely in her three-cornered contest.

A few days later (23 July) the parliamentary party elected a new front bench, placing Gordon Brown first, followed by Tony Blair and Robin Cook. Four women were also elected, and four more were high among the 'also-rans'. Smith immediately made Margaret Beckett shadow Leader of the House and Campaign Co-ordinator. Gordon Brown became shadow Chancellor with Harriet Harman as his deputy; Jack Cunningham was appointed shadow Foreign Secretary and Tony Blair shadow Home Secretary. Robin Cook moved from Health to Trade and Industry, but John Prescott remained at Transport, ready to attack Government plans to privatise British Rail. Health was to be looked after by David Blunkett, the former leader of Sheffield Council. This was a team well-equipped to provide a strong opposition to a Government by no means as strong as Mrs Thatcher's had been.

FURTHER READING

On the two general elections of 1987 and 1992, see D. E. Butler and D. Kavanagh, *British General Election of 1987* (1988) and *British General Election of 1992* (1992); also I. Crewe and M. Harrop, *Political Communications: The General Election Campaign of 1987* (Cambridge, 1989). For the decline of extremism in the party membership — as well as its numerical decline — see P. Seyd and P. Whiteley, *Labour's Grassroots* (Oxford, 1992). Eric Shaw, *Discipline and Discord in the Labour Party* (1988) deals with the formation of the National Constitutional Committee. On the campaign to retain the union political funds, see K. Coates and T. Topham, *Trade Unions and Politics* (Oxford, 1986) and Andrew Taylor, *The Trade Unions and the Labour Party* (1987).

CHAPTER XIII

Conclusion: The Past and the Future

ALTHOUGH political parties possess a certain organic character, it is not easy to analyse their structure in precise biological terms, or to predict their processes of adaptation or decay. The Labour Party, although unique in many ways, is no exception in this respect. Many of the generalisations that may be attempted to describe its effective working and development soon come to need qualification; and forecasts of its future behaviour must be tentative in character.

The party was founded to represent a class interest in Parliament, and its formal tie both with the trade unions and with the Socialists reflects this fact. And yet right from the start it began to pick up many of the traditional features of Liberalism, usually regarded as the ethos of the middle class: the support of religious Nonconformity, the advocacy of Free Trade, the creed of internationalism of the Bright and Cobden variety. During and after the First World War the Liberal Party began to disintegrate, and the Liberal intellectuals began to move over to the Labour Party, thus perpetuating the tendency of the party to find its support to some extent across, rather than within, the boundaries of class.

Originally, the control of the party depended a good deal upon the efforts of the most enthusiastic supporters of the 'Labour Alliance' — the I.L.P. leaders, and particularly Ramsay MacDonald, who was the party secretary. Arthur Henderson, who succeeded MacDonald as secretary, also had his period of almost unchallenged authority. But the annual conference was always important, and its public debates, unlike those of the National Liberal Federation or the National Union of Conservative Associations, resulted in decisions that normally became binding upon the party as a whole. In time, however, the parliamentary party asserted more and more discretion for itself; and the smooth running of the whole organisation, and a reasonable degree of harmony between leadership and Conference, came to depend upon effective liaison between the parliamentary leaders and those trade-union officials who wielded the largest block votes at Conference.

This liaison of parliamentary and trade-union leaders was not easy to maintain, especially when the parliamentary party grew in size and came within reach of power; and it was hindered by the fact that the major trade-union leaders since the 1920's have been too preoccupied with their union duties and with membership of the T.U.C. General Council to maintain constant contact with parliamentary affairs. Thus it was that the conflict of Ramsay MacDonald and the General Council of the T.U.C. in 1931 was preceded by several years in which liaison had been slight and unfriendly. It was in an effort to overcome this difficulty that the National Council of Labour was set up on a new basis in 1932: but the situation of that time, with a shrunken and ineffective parliamentary leadership, meant that Bevin and Citrine for a few years controlled the parliamentary party by a curious 'indirect rule'. Later on, the apparently pliant Attlee — a master of the *coup de repos* — won Bevin's confidence, and a period of good relations ensued that lasted until 1950. Only after Attlee's retirement did the liaison again prove unsatisfactory, partly as a result of Gaitskell's attempt to force the pace of constitutional reform within the party, and partly owing to the accident that the mantle of Bevin fell upon a militant of the Left in Frank Cousins.

Whether the union leadership, when and if it recovers its unity of view, will again dominate the party, is open to doubt. After 1958, when the T.U.C. moved its headquarters from Transport House to Bloomsbury, its links with the party were somewhat reduced. In 1960 the *Daily Herald* (now the

Sun) was for financial reasons released from the position of dependence on the T.U.C. devised by Ernest Bevin. Also, the trade-union leaders lost public esteem as it became clear that they had failed to set their own house in order. But the Trade Union Group of M.P.s remained by no means a negligible force, as they showed in 1969; the Transport Workers remained the landlord of the Labour Party; and in the early 1970s the fight against the Conservative Industrial Relations Act drew the unions and the party together again in the new T.U.C.-Labour Party Liaison Committee — an instrument that the Labour leadership still finds valuable in its search for a policy of wage restraint.

Meanwhile, modern techniques of mass communication, especially television, have strengthened the importance of the party leader, especially when he is Prime Minister. But his position is still one that requires the art of diplomacy in order to keep the peace between the parliamentary party and the National Executive. Harold Wilson, like Attlee, before becoming leader made a great point of loyalty to the decisions of the party conference. After he became Prime Minister he faced, owing to external circumstances, severe challenges to his authority: it was to his credit that he mastered them, and ensured that on most of the important questions decided under his leadership both the conference and the National Executive were loyal to him, rather than the other way about.

James Callaghan sought to retain control in the same way, and for over two years appeared to be succeeding. But the election defeat of 1979 was followed by a strong demand for constitutional reform within the party, in order to subject the Leader to the control of the National Executive, and the parliamentary party to the wishes of local management committees. Although Michael Foot, who succeeded Callaghan in 1980, was both a left-winger and a staunch defender of the independence of the parliamentary party, he could not prevent the new Left, under Tony Benn, from asserting itself aggressively, nor avoid a right-wing secession backed by four former Cabinet Ministers and a total of twenty-nine M.P.s.

The defeats that Labour suffered in the 1983 and 1987 elections were due partly to this secession and partly to continuing divisions within the party. Nevertheless, it appeared in the 1990s that the old two-party system was re-asserting itself, although the Kinnock–Hattersley leadership was unable fully to recover the ground that had been lost, especially in London, the South of England and the Midlands. It remained to be seen whether a new opportunity would arise under the new leadership. At least Kinnock could claim to have re-united the party, as had been hoped of him in 1983.

APPENDIX A

PARTY MEMBERSHIP

Date	Individual Membership	T.U. Member-ship	Co-operative Societies Member-ship*	Socialist Societies etc. Membership	Total
1900–1	Nil	353,070	Nil	22,861	375,931
1901–2	Nil	455,450	Nil	13,861	469,311
1902–3	Nil	847,315	Nil	13,835	861,150
1903–4	Nil	956,025	Nil	13,775	969,800
1904–5	Nil	855,270	Nil	14,730	900,000
1905–6	Nil	904,496	Nil	16,784	921,280
1906–7	Nil	975,182	2,271	20,885	998,338
1907	Nil	1,049,673	472	22,267	1,072,413†
1908	Nil	1,127,035	565	27,465	1,158,565
1909	Nil	1,450,648	678	30,982	1,486,308
1910	Nil	1,394,403	760	31,377	1,430,539
1911	Nil	1,501,783	911	31,404	1,539,092
1912	Nil	1,858,178	1,073	31,237	1,895,498
1913	Nil	Not compiled‡	1,328	33,304	Not compiled‡
1914	Nil	1,572,391	1,526	33,230	1,612,147
1915	Nil	2,053,735	1,792	32,828	2,093,365
1916	Nil	2,170,782	1,792	42,190	2,219,764
1917	Nil	2,415,383	2,608	47,140	2,465,131
1918	Not compiled	2,960,409	Nil	52,720	3,013,129
1919	,,	3,464,020	Nil	47,270	3,511,290
1920	,,	4,317,537	Nil	42,270	4,359,807
1921	,,	3,973,558	Nil	36,803	4,010,361
1922	,,	3,279,276	Nil	31,760	3,311,036
1923	,,	3,120,149	Nil	35,762	3,155,911
1924	,,	3,158,002	Nil	36,397	3,194,399
1925	,,	3,337,635	Nil	36,235	3,373,870
1926	,,	3,352,347	Nil	35,939	3,388,286
1927	,,	3,238,939	20,000	34,676	3,293,615
1928	214,970	2,025,139	20,000	32,060	2,292,169
1929	227,897	2,044,279	32,000	26,669	2,330,845
1930	277,211	2,011,484	32,000	26,213	2,346,908
1931	297,003	2,024,216	32,000	4,847	2,358,066
1932	371,607	1,960,269	32,040	7,871	2,371,787
1933	366,013	1,899,007	32,040	7,970	2,305,030
1934	381,259	1,857,524	22,040	7,667	2,278,490
1935	419,311	1,912,924	36,000	9,280	2,377,515
1936	430,694	1,968,538	36,000	9,125	2,444,357

Appendix A: Party Membership—contd.

Date	Individual Membership	T.U. Membership	Co-operative Societies Membership*	Socialist Societies etc. Membership	Total
1937	447,150	2,037,071	37,333	6,118	2,527,672
1938	428,826	2,158,076	37,333	6,054	2,630,286
1939	408,844	2,214,070	37,333	2,820	2,663,067
1940	404,124	2,226,575	37,333	3,131	2,571,163
1941	226,622	2,230,728	25,200	2,908	2,485,458
1942	218,783	2,206,209	25,200	3,740	2,453,932
1943	235,501	2,237,307	25,200	5,232	2,503,240
1944	265,763	2,375,381	25,200	6,501	2,672,845
1945	487,047	2,510,369	33,600	7,681	3,038,697
1946	645,345	2,635,346	33,600	8,067	3,322,358
1947	608,487	4,386,074	36,960	8,778	5,040,299
1948	629,025	4,751,030	33,600	8,782	5,422,437
1949	729,624	4,946,207	33,600	7,516	5,716,947
1950	908,161	4,971,911	30,800	9,300	5,920,172
1951	876,275	4,937,427	28,000	7,300	5,849,002
1952	1,014,524	5,071,935	14,000	7,200	6,107,659
1953	1,004,685	5,056,912	28,000	7,425	6,096,022
1954	933,657	5,529,760	28,000	7,610	6,498,027
1955	843,356	5,605,988	28,000	7,650	6,483,994
1956	845,129	5,658,249	28,000	6,850	6,537,228
1957	912,987	5,644,012	20,000	5,550	6,582,549
1958	888,955	5,627,690	20,000	5,541	6,542,186
1959	847,526	5,564,010	20,000	5,540	6,436,986
1960	790,192	5,512,688	20,000	5,450	6,328,330
1961	750,565	5,549,592	20,000	5,450	6,325,607
1962	767,459	5,502,773	20,000	5,475	6,295,707
1963	830,346	5,507,232	16,000	4,858	6,358,436
1964	830,116	5,502,001	16,000	5,200	6,353,317
1965	816,765	5,601,982	16,000	5,146	6,439,893
1966	675,693	5,538,744	16,000	5,175	6,335,612
1967	733,932	5,539,562	16,000	5,120	6,294,614
1968	700,856	5,364,484	16,000	5,285	6,086,625
1969	680,656	5,461,721	16,000	5,505	6,163,882
1970	680,191	5,518,520	16,000	7,869	6,222,580
1971	699,522	5,559,371	17,000	8,360	6,284,253
1972	703,030	5,425,327	17,000	23,415	6,168,772
1973	665,379	5,364,904	17,000	25,913	6,073,196
1974	691,889	5,787,467	19,000	20,101	6,518,457
1975	674,905	5,750,039	43,930		6,468,874
1976	659,058	5,800,069	48,210		6,459,127
1977	659,737	5,913,159	43,375		6,616,271
1978	675,946	6,259,595	54,623		6,990,164
1979	660,091	6,511,179	58,328		7,235,598
1980	348,156¶	6,406,914	56,200		6,811,270
1981	276,692	6,273,292	57,606		6,607,590
1982	273,803	6,185,063	57,131		6,515,997

Appendix A: Party Membership—contd.

Date	Individual Membership	T.U. Membership	Co-operative Societies Membership*	Socialist Societies etc. Membership	Total
1983	295,344	6,101,438	58,955		6,455,737
1984	323,292	5,843,586	60,163		6,227,041
1985	313,099	5,827,479	59,581		6,200,159
1986	297,364	5,778,184	57,762		6,133,310
1987	288,829	5,564,477	54,843		5,908,149
1988	265,927	5,481,764	56,205		5,803,896
1989	293,723	5,335,764	52,913		5,682,400
1990	311,152	4,923,952	54,167		5,287,271
1991	261,233	4,811,280	53,612		5,126,125

* This does not include the membership of the Co-operative Party (founded in 1917).

† The totals between 1907 and 1917 in this column also include membership of the Women's Labour League.

‡ Trade-union membership figures could not be compiled for 1913 owing to the operation of the Osborne Judgment.

¶ New basis for calculation.

APPENDIX B

GENERAL ELECTION RESULTS

Date	Seats Contested	Members Returned	Total Votes Polled
1900	15	2	63,304
1906	50	29	323,195
1910 (Jan.)	78	40	505,657
1910 (Dec.)	56	42	371,772
1918	361	57	2,244,945
1922	411	142	4,241,383
1923	422	191	4,438,508
1924	512	151	5,489,077
1929	571	288	8,389,512
1931	491	46	6,362,561
1935	552	154	8,325,491
1945	604	393	11,995,152
1950	617	315	13,266,592
1951	617	295	13,948,605
1955	620	277	12,404,970
1959	621	258	12,215,538
1964	628	317	12,205,606
1966	621	363	13,064,951
1970	624	287	12,179,341
1974 (Feb.)	623	301	11,639,243
1974 (Oct.)	623	319	11,457,079
1979	623	269	11,532,148
1983	633	209	8,457,124
1987	633	229	10,029,270
1992	634	271	11,559,735

APPENDIX C

CHAIRMEN AND LEADERS OF THE PARLIAMENTARY PARTY

Note—In 1922 the designation was changed from 'Chairman' to 'Chairman and Leader'. In 1970 the posts of 'Chairman' and 'Leader' were entirely separated, and only the 'Leader' is listed here.

1906–8	J. Keir Hardie
1908–10	Arthur Henderson
1910–11	George Barnes
1911–14	J. Ramsay MacDonald
1914–17	Arthur Henderson
1917–21	W. Adamson
1921–22	J. R. Clynes
1922–31	J. Ramsay MacDonald
1931–32	Arthur Henderson (Leader only)
1931–35	George Lansbury
1935–55	C. R. Attlee
1955–63	Hugh Gaitskell
1963–76	Harold Wilson
1976–80	James Callaghan
1980–83	Michael Foot
1983–92	Neil Kinnock
1992–	John Smith

APPENDIX D

PARTY SECRETARIES

1900–12	J. Ramsay MacDonald
1912–34	Arthur Henderson
1935–44	J. S. Middleton
1944–61	Morgan Phillips
1962–68	Len Williams
1968–72	H. R. Nicholas
1972–82	Ron Hayward
1982–85	Jim Mortimer
1985–	Larry Whitty

INDEX

Index

Index

Gordon Walker, Patrick, 131, 133, 134
Gould, Bryan, 192, 193, 200
Grayson, Victor, 22, 23, 24
Greene, Ben, 83
Greenwood, Anthony, 132, 135
Greenwood, Arthur, 79, 81, 89, 90, 96, 111, 112
Grey, Sir Edward, 29, 35, 37
Griffiths, James, 98, 117
Guild Socialism, 26, 44 f.
Gunter, Ray, 143

Haig, Alexander, 182
Haldane, Lord, 56, 64
Halifax, Lord, 84, 86
Hardie, J. Keir, I. L. P. leader, 4, 7, 10, 13, 14, 15, 24, 29, 32, 35; Labour Party chairman, 20, 21; distrusts union leader, 21, 22, 23
Harman, Harriet, 201
Hart, Mrs. Judith, 166
Hattersley, Roy, 168, 186 f., 193, 196, 200, 205
Hayward, Ron, 154, 157, 164, 165
Healey, Denis, 131, 162, 168, 170, 171, 175, 176, 179, 181, 185, 186, 187, 193
Heath, Edward, 125, 136, 137, 139, 151, 154, 157, 160, 163, 164, 165, 169
Heffer, Eric, 166, 186
Henderson, Arthur, early career, 14, 20, 21 f., 32 f.; party leader (1914–22), 35–50, 202; Foreign Secretary, 64–6; resumes leadership (1931–2), 67, 71, 72, 75; other refs., 53, 55, 56, 63, 78
Herald. See *Daily Herald*
Herriot, E., 57
Heseltine, Michael, 198
Hirst, Stanley, 68, 72
Hitler, Adolf, 78, 84, 85
Hobson, J. A., 62
Hodge, John, 14, 39
Home, Lord. See Douglas-Home, Sir Alec
Horner, Arthur, 101 f.
Houghton Committee, 170
Housing Act (1924), 57
Housing Finance Act (1972), 156, 163
Howe, Sir Geoffrey, 157 f., 195
Howell, Denis, 146
Hull by-election (1966), 136
Hussein, Saddam, 196–7
Hyndman, H. M., 25

Independent Labour Party (I.L.P.), as constituent of the Labour Party, 4, 7–10, 13, 15, 30, 198; internal dissension in, 22, 24; opposes First World War, 37, 38, 39 f., 44, 46; becomes resort of the Left, 50, 54 f., 56, 57, 59,

62 f.; in conflict with Labour Party, 66, 74, 75 f., 83; decline, 76, 81
India, 65, 100 f.
Indian National Congress, 65
Industrial Relations Act (1971), 157–9, 160, 161, 162, 204
Industry Act (1975), 168
In Place of Strife (1969), 144
International, Socialist, 28 f., 35, 41; Communist, 62, 82, 84
International Justice, Permanent Court of, 65 f.
International Monetary Fund, 168
Ireland, 3, 49, 148, 153, 156
Irish Home Rule, 15, 28, 30, 33
Irish Nationalist Party, 4, 19, 35
Iron and Steel Federation, 119
Iron and steel, nationalisation of, 97, 102, 106, 114, 119, 147
Ironfounders, Friendly Society of, 14, 32
Israel, 101, 142, 159

Jenkins, Roy, 142, 143, 144, 145, 149, 154, 155–6, 162, 163, 167, 179 f., 182, 186
Johnston, Thomas, 64, 90, 92
Jolly George, 47
Jones, Jack, 166
Jowett, Fred, 56, 64
Jowitt, Sir William, 89

Kaufman, Gerald, 187, 193, 196, 200
'Keep Left' group, 99 f., 102, 109
Keynes, J. M., 62, 69
Keys, Bill, 190
King, Dr. Horace, 137
King, Tom, 188
Kinnock, Neil, 186 f., 189–196, 200, 205
Korean War, 107

Labour, National Council of. See National Joint Council
Labour and the Nation (1928), 63, 65
Labour and the New Social Order (1918), 44, 63
Labour Believes in Britain (1950), 102
Labour Coordinating Committee, 176
Labour Electoral Committee, 8
Labour Government, First, (1924), 56–9; Second (1929–31), 64–7; Third (1945–51), 88, 95–103, 106–108; Fourth (1964–70), 124 f., 131–51; Fifth (1974–9), 153, 161–170
Labour Party (*originally* Labour Representation Committee), constitution, 8 f., 12 f., 43–5, *and see* Clause Four, local or divisional parties of, 13, 30, 31, 43, 44, 46, 53 f., 55, 63, 83, 105, 110,

Index

Index